D0780089

CLARISSA'S CIPHERS

CLARISSA'S CIPHERS

Meaning & Disruption in Richardson's "Clarissa"

TERRY CASTLE

CORNELL UNIVERSITY PRESS

Ithaca and London

First published 1982 by Cornell University Press.
Published in the United Kingdom by Cornell University Press Ltd.,
Ely House, 37 Dover Street, London W1X 4HQ.

International Standard Book Number 0-8014-1495-4
Library of Congress Catalog Card Number 82-2460
Printed in the United States of America

*Librarians: Library of Congress cataloging information
appears on the last page of the book.*

*The paper in this book is acid-free, and meets
the guidelines for permanence and durability of the
Committee on Production Guidelines for Book
Longevity of the Council on Library Resources.*

For my mother and Turk

Contents

Figures

Acknowledgments

I am grateful to those who have given me their advice, encouragement, and friendship while I have been working on this book. My greatest debt—much larger than a single note can acknowledge—is to Paul Alkon, who has overseen this project since its beginning. His support has been unfailing, his enthusiasm sustaining, his commentary invaluable. Madelon Gohlke, Robert E. Moore, Chester Anderson, and Janet Spector all offered many helpful criticisms during the early stages of this work, and recently I have benefited much from the useful suggestions and goodwill of Margaret Doody, Robert Hume, and Ronald Paulson. Nancy K. Miller has shared with me her insights, friendship, and critical *savoir faire*. I owe thanks to the Department of English at the University of Minnesota and the Bush Foundation for supporting me during the first part of this project, and to Burton Dreben and the Society of Fellows at Harvard University for generously providing me with a new and stimulating milieu in which to carry on my work. I am grateful to Basil Blackwell Publisher for permission to reprint quotations and to reproduce two pages from the Shakespeare Head Press edition of *Clarissa* (Oxford, 1943). Finally—for reasons as multifarious as they are deeply felt—

ACKNOWLEDGMENTS

thank you to Nancy Reinhardt, Kristin Midelfort, Dennis Allen, Frieda Gardner, Malka Goodman, Richard Garner, Peter Galison, and my friends and colleagues in the Society of Fellows.

TERRY CASTLE

Cambridge, Massachusetts

CLARISSA'S CIPHERS

Introduction

One might imagine the present book as gloss for a single line of *Clarissa*. "I am but a *cypher*, to give *him* significance, and *myself* pain." The words are Clarissa's, written at Sinclair's, in the midst of her evil time. And "he" of course is Lovelace—jailer, bogey, courtier—fixer of that intimate, brutal anguish she is made to suffer. Clarissa leaves her remark unexplained, almost a throwaway line. It is subsumed in a plangent cry of grief to Anna Howe, the only friend, it seems, who will not "grudge" her her sadness. Yet Clarissa's startling image—the body as cipher—stays with the reader. Once again, as so often in reading *Clarissa*, we may feel the heroine has said more than she knows.

And indeed, what has she said? Clarissa's words register distress. They mark the fact of pain. They also figure, however, the dialectic of pain. In the midst of crisis, Clarissa finds a trope—a syllepsis—for catastrophe. Uncovering the crucial metaphor of reading, she stumbles, half-consciously, on a precise symbol for her bondage. She has become a cipher to Lovelace, a sort of text—and he, her exegete. "Clarissa Harlowe" is but a sign—the letter—from which, obscurely, he takes away significance. She herself receives nothing from this act of penetration—nothing, that is, except grief. She remains the subject of his interpretation, without pleasure or power as such: a hermeneutic casualty.

This book is an attempt to elaborate Clarissa's fateful metaphor, to measure the range of its power, both within and without *Clarissa*. The heroine's trope has a twofold interest, it seems to me: for how we approach the inner drama of the novel—and Clarissa's peculiar, wrenching *agon*—and for our own relationship to Richardson's massive, yet often baffling text. Clarissa remains a "cypher" to those who surround her in the fictional world, a subject for countless interpreters. With only a few exceptions, the interpretations others place on her are variously self-serving, banal, unjust. They have tragic consequences. But the fiction bearing her name, Richardson's beguiling, fragmented "History of a Young Lady," is another sort of cipher. It opens itself equally to interpretation, that of real readers. I have been concerned here, above all, to enlarge on this fundamental correspondence—to say what it might mean to decipher, both inside the fiction and outside. My subject is the matter of exegesis: how it operates within *Clarissa*, both as a mode of human contact and as a mode of violence, the ways in which it may be said to condition the heroine's fate, and ultimately, how this internal revelation affects reading outside the text, our confrontation with the fiction itself.

Clarissa's remarkable form—the intricate, clumsy, strangely beautiful "Epistolary Manner of Writing"—allows for such movement between inner and outer dimensions of the text. It invites a jump between levels. Indeed, the unique power of Richardson's justly celebrated epistolary mode is that it creates the illusion of a palimpsest of reading. There are at once decipherers within the fiction—the myriad correspondents who, through the medium of the letter, swerve together, argue, flirt, cajole, and torment each other—and decipherers without, real readers: anyone willing to plunge into the vast "Series of Letters" and pull out of it Clarissa's "Story." By its form *Clarissa* simultaneously alludes to hundreds of fictional acts of interpretation and demands still another—our own.

Traditionally, criticism of Samuel Richardson's masterpiece has turned upon either inner or outer dimension—on specific aspects of "content" or "form," "plot" or "style." Since Richardson's own day, a plethora of readers and critics have tried to say exactly what goes on "inside" *Clarissa*. Not least among these was the author himself, who, even before he had finished composing, had begun to explain to anyone who would listen what he intended to convey in the fiction. *Clarissa* was to be his revelation of "the highest and most important Doctrines not only of Morality, but of Christianity," and its heroine "an Exemplar to her Sex."[1] But similarly, from Diderot to Dorothy Van Ghent, a host of interpreters have explicated the "cypher" posed by the novel—by delineating, first of all, what the heroine's puzzling "Story" in fact *is*, and beyond this, what it all *means*.

Paralleling the discussion of *Clarissa*'s meaning, but seldom intersecting with it, has been an extended discussion of form, and of the uses of the epistolary mode as narrative technique. Treatments of form in the novel have usually been historical in nature—focusing, variously, on Richardson's reasons for choosing the epistolary "Manner," its literary provenance and prototypes, the relation between the strategies and ideology of fictional correspondence and those of actual correspondence in the eighteenth century, or (as in Ian Watt's classic discussion in *The Rise of the Novel*) on those more intangible cultural and intellectual changes that made the letter form seem to contemporary readers an eminently plausible and indeed preferred mode of narrative art.

1. Preface, *Clarissa*. All references are to the Shakespeare Head Press edition of the novel, 8 vols. (Oxford: Basil Blackwell, 1943). Parenthetical notations following quotations show volume and page number.

What has been missing until very lately has been an investigation of the basic link between "inside" and "outside" in *Clarissa,* between story and shape: the matter of interpretation itself. Even in several excellent studies that, emerging in the mid-1970s, heralded a reinvigoration of Richardson scholarship (Mark Kinkead-Weekes's *Samuel Richardson: Dramatic Novelist* and Margaret Doody's *A Natural Passion: A Study of the Novels of Samuel Richardson,* for example), the issue of hermeneutics is not really raised. Kinkead-Weekes sees the complicated epistolary transactions going on throughout *Clarissa* as a formal analogue to the "dramatic" psychological interplay between characters, but does not explore specifically the significance of those fictionalized gestures of interpretation which at once motivate and are recorded in the epistolary sequence. What these might have to do with Clarissa's shocking "Story"—or indeed with the role of the real reader—is left unexamined. Margaret Doody's work, again, has been primarily historical in approach, more concerned with the contemporary iconographic dimensions of certain scenic moments in the text than with hermeneutic issues.[2]

The most recent commentary on *Clarissa* may represent, however, a shift in critical focus. A short yet prescient essay by John Preston in *The Created Self: The Reader's Role in Eighteenth-Century Fiction* suggests a different direction for scholarship on the novel by proposing a new thematics for consideration: the function of the written artifact in the fiction, the ontological status of the letter itself. In a similar vein, William B. Warner takes up and develops the subject of reading in *Reading Clarissa: The Struggles of Interpretation.*[3]

2. Mark Kinkead-Weekes, *Samuel Richardson: Dramatic Novelist* (Ithaca: Cornell University Press, 1973); Margaret Doody, *A Natural Passion: A Study of the Novels of Samuel Richardson* (London: Oxford University Press at the Clarendon Press, 1974).
    3. John Preston, *The Created Self: The Reader's Role in Eighteenth-Century Fiction* (London: Heinemann, 1970); William B. Warner, *Reading Clarissa:*

Introduction

Richardson criticism has begun to reflect, finally, the work of European scholars on the epistolary novel generally—in particular the theoretical investigations of Tzvetan Todorov and François Jost.[4] I place my own examination of hermeneutic questions raised by *Clarissa* in the context of this larger discussion.

In what follows I begin inside, with what one could call the thematicization of interpretation, that drama of exegesis to which the great chain of correspondence alludes. In a technical sense, of course, everyone in *Clarissa* is an exegete; everyone is caught up in a world of "cyphers." Clarissa, Lovelace, Anna, Belford and the rest—these characters are present to us first as readers of texts: they exist in that they participate in a vast system of epistolary exchange. Their own letters preserve interpretations of previous texts: those of their correspondents. Thus the letter, the basic textual unit in *Clarissa*, is a *writing* which is also, paradoxically, a *reading*. It registers its author's acts of textual exegesis.

But Richardson's correspondents are readers in another, larger sense. They are decipherers of the great "Book of Nature" itself. As many commentators have pointed out, that "writing to the moment" in which characters in the fiction obsessively engage is weighted with phenomenological impor-

---

The Struggles of Interpretation (New Haven: Yale University Press, 1979). Warner's study (which came to my attention as I finished the first draft of this manuscript) shares certain methodological assumptions with my own. We reach, however, very different conclusions regarding the internal drama of reading in *Clarissa*. For an extended discussion of Warner's book, see the Bibliographic Postscript.

4. See, for example, Todorov's "The Discovery of Language: *Les Liaisons dangereuses* and *Adolphe*," *Yale French Studies*, 45 (1970), 113–26, as well as François Jost's "Le Roman épistolaire et la technique narrative au XVIIIe siècle," *Comparative Literature Studies*, 3 (1966), 397–427, and "L'Evolution d'un genre: le roman épistolaire dans les lettres occidentales," in *Essais de littérature comparée*, vol. 2 (Fribourg: Editions Universitaires, 1964).

tance: it represents an ongoing effort to inscribe a vision—an interpretation—of the world. The prolific "scribbling" of Clarissa, Lovelace, and the others reflects a will to define experience, to transform the elusive moment into discourse. Letter writing is always existentially motivated in *Clarissa*. To borrow Patricia Meyer Spacks' phrase, it is a way of "imagining a self": of capturing the truth of the personal, suspending oneself and one's sense of things—in language.[5]

What *Clarissa* reveals, however, is that this great project shared by each fictional correspondent—the inscription of subjective experience—is a shockingly compromised (and compromising) activity. It is fraught with dangers, and thrusts one into complex, potentially destructive human transactions. This revelation has several layers. The basic form of reading going on within the fictional world, actual textual interpretation, is, first of all, a curiously suspect and arbitrary operation. Letters fail to disclose transparent meanings in *Clarissa*: again and again we watch readers construe them variously— misreading according to desires and prejudices, extracting private meanings, none of which may have anything to do with the letter writer's intentions. Estranged from its authorial source, the letter becomes a profoundly indeterminate structure: it conveys no essential significance, but allows itself to be perused creatively—its "Hints" drawn out, its meaning(s) supplied—by its reader. Letters elicit multiple interpretations; each new reader may decipher differently.

This indeterminacy is always paradigmatic, however, for the text of human experience itself is likewise lacking in transparency. The significance of human actions in *Clarissa* does not inhere, seemingly, in the actions themselves, but is promoted, retroactively, by interpreters, those who witness and

---

5. Patricia Meyer Spacks, *Imagining a Self: Autobiography and Novel in Eighteenth-Century England* (Cambridge, Mass.: Harvard University Press, 1976).

comment on action. Characters in *Clarissa* insistently make
"constructions"—of letters, of each other, and finally of Nature itself.[6] These "constructions" tend to subsume the realm
of events, to become events in themselves. The great "Book"
of human nature comes into being, paradoxically, as it is deciphered; in explicating, Richardson's characters define the
"cyphers" that surround them. They read into the world,
shape its significance actively, according to their lights. To use
Lovelace's favorite dichotomy, the "Art" of the exegete re-
places the "Nature" of experience.

The tragedy is that this opacity in the realm of events, the
inaccessibility of any single human truth, breeds a kind of
hermeneutic anarchy. The license with which *Clarissa*'s readers
read meaning into things (and into each other) has violent
consequences. A ground for human conflict opens up. The
fiction is just *this*, after all: a cacophony of voices, a multiplicity of exegetes struggling to articulate different "constructions" of the world. Clarissa and Lovelace obviously are the
most important of these antagonists: through the crucial
medium of the letter, each strives to voice an interpretation of
events, each other, and of the grotesque, convulsive sexual
dynamic in which they are caught. As Clarissa sometimes
suspects, their "constructions" are painfully at odds, "different in *essentials.*" For Clarissa reads naively, deciphering
both letter and experience by dint of a compulsive benevolism.
She reads into Lovelace, for instance, a sincerity that is not
there, a susceptibility to imminent reformation. Blindly she
falls victim to Lovelace's forgeries and stratagems, his parodies
of authenticity. He, on the other hand, holds the nature of

6. Throughout this book certain key words—"construction," "penetration," "cypher," "authority," "Art," and the like—appear in double quotes, at
once to mark their origination in the Richardsonian text and to give them
special emphasis. Rich in potential meaning, these words carry talismanic
force for Richardson's characters, and they should carry a similar force, I
think, for *Clarissa*'s readers.

things to be deceptive, sullied, everywhere open to corruption—including, cynically enough, the "Angel" Clarissa herself. With its abrupt shifts and jerks, the epistolary text mimics the underlying semantic struggle between them: the real reader receives the "constructions" first of one, then the other. Epistemologically speaking, our perspective on the fictional world is dialectical.

The conflict of "constructions" thematized within *Clarissa*—revealed most starkly by the textual juxtaposition of Clarissa's "whitened" and Lovelace's "blackened" glosses on each other—does not remain simply epistemological: it quickly becomes a political struggle. And as I try to show here in some detail, it is a conflict in which Clarissa, the child-woman, is inevitably the loser. She is "broken" by it. Throughout this book I will maintain not only that Clarissa's experience is fundamentally tragic, but that her tragic status is inseparable from her representation, within Richardson's fiction, as an exemplary victim of hermeneutic violence. Across the text, hers is that voice which repeatedly fails to make itself heard.

Clarissa's victimization is figured several ways. At the most primitive level, she is excluded from speech by those around her. She must struggle to speak, to tell her own "Story." This "Story"—the one Anna requests in the first letter of *Clarissa*—is doomed to suppression, interruption, incompletion. At Harlowe-Place and again at Mrs. Sinclair's brothel, Clarissa is "shut up" in two senses: she is imprisoned by those who wield power over her, and she is also subject to various acts of silencing: interruption when she tries to speak out, prohibition of her correspondence, interception and violation of those letters she does manage to write clandestinely (as when Lovelace tampers with the letters to and from Anna), and finally that literal silencing—crudely, by an opiate—which results in the violation of her body itself. In contrast, the rights of her oppressors to language go unquestioned.

Introduction

Lovelace's powers of expression, for instance, are not subject to limit. Unlike his victim, he has control over what one might call the basic "modes of production" in the epistolary world— free access to pens, paper, and so on. Moreover, he has the wherewithal, the prestige, to send letters openly, to disrupt the correspondence of others, to exploit the system of exchange. What Roland Barthes has written of the very different relations to language exhibited by libertine and victim in the Marquis de Sade's novels might apply equally to Lovelace and Clarissa. "Aside from murder there is but one trait the libertines themselves possess and never share, in any form whatever: speech. The master is he who speaks, who disposes of the entirety of language; the object is [one] who is silent, who remains separate, by a mutilation more absolute than any erotic torture, from any access to discourse."[7] Again, witnessing Clarissa's predicament, we may be reminded of one of Simone Weil's characteristic observations—"the basic loss of the afflicted is the loss of the voice."[8]

Clarissa's struggle for language marks off at a basic level, however, the nature of her larger struggle: to make meaning itself out of her experience, to articulate a reading of events. In the midst of duress, she preserves a will to interpret. She wants to *understand* the horrific and bizarre dislocations she is being made to endure. Her will to "make sense," however, leads her further into trouble: she is everywhere poignantly susceptible to those various deceitful texts—both literal and figurative—"written" and presented to her by Lovelace, the "author of her sufferings." Lovelace plays neatly on the heroine's frustrated (and preeminently naive) desire to "con-

7. Roland Barthes, *Sade—Fourier—Loyola*, trans. Richard Miller (New York: Hill & Wang, 1976), p. 31.
8. Michelle Cliff, "The Resonance of Interruption," *Chrysalis: A Magazine of Women's Culture*, no. 8 (1979), 29–37. See also Simone Weil's essay "Human Personality" in *The Simone Weil Reader*, ed. George A. Panichas (New York: David McKay, 1977).

struct" meaning by thrusting her repeatedly into uncanny situations that invite her interpretation. She invariably does so incorrectly, however, for he sets up her readings in advance, anticipates her responses, controls the way she sees things. The libertine takes charge of what Barthes, again speaking of Sade's novels, calls the "direction of meaning." In the protracted critical scenes at Mrs. Sinclair's, therefore, when Clarissa works to make sense of the upsetting, surreal events in which she is caught, the results are disastrous: Lovelace has already manipulated those signs she attempts to decipher, and has shaped her conclusions ahead of time—to his own advantage.

At the same time that Clarissa's own acts of interpretation are constrained by others, she is also, as I suggested at the outset, a text for everyone else's maniacal, irrepressible exegesis—their "cypher." According to their enigmatic desires, the Harlowes inscribe her with a range of oppressive meanings: "ungrateful" daughter, "perverse" sister, "fallen" woman. For Lovelace of course she is the reification of his banal fantasy "Woman"—weak, hypersexual, secretly enamored of the machinations of the "Rakish Confraternity." None of these readings of the heroine has any necessary connection to the body in question; Lovelace's infantile fiction of "Woman," for instance, has nothing to do with Clarissa, the woman. Each is strictly a function of private vision. Yet she is powerless to contravert these "constructions" of her nature—a hermeneutic victim.

In *Reading Clarissa* William B. Warner has written eloquently of the "struggles of interpretation" taking place between Clarissa and Lovelace. One must disagree with his central claim, however, that the heroine's interpretative gestures represent a "powerful rhetorical system evolved to meet the exigencies of the struggle her life has become."[9] The ex-

9. Warner, p. 268.

cruciating situation *Clarissa* dramatizes is that a rhetorical system is *not* "powerful" unless grounded in political power. Clarissa's "Story" everywhere lacks underlying authority. It is without social and material force. Hence it remains a fragmentary, futile utterance subject to the radical incursions of a more potent collective rhetoric—the patriarchal discourse of the Harlowes and Lovelace.

Clarissa's vulnerability to Lovelace's rhetorical affronts and semantic deceptions must be linked ultimately to the sexual exploitation she suffers at his hands. As she revolts, albeit vainly, against what is being done to her, the inner drama of reading moves inexorably to its tragic close. Her rape is the most chilling consequence of that hermeneutic conflict shaping *Clarissa*. It elaborates, on the plane of the physical, the semantic violation she has already suffered. For by the act of sexual violence Lovelace enforces his "construction" of the heroine *directly* upon her. He penetrates the "cypher" in the most bitter manner possible. Rape is the crowning proof of his thesis, the despicable yet perversely logical extension of his reading of her. As such, this "black transaction" at the heart of the text confirms the political shape of the struggle between them. In *Clarissa*'s bleak inner landscape, those constructions prevail which are grounded in power, a capacity to brutalize—what Lovelace blandly calls "force." Clarissa is without force: as a woman she is without the kinds of power available to Lovelace—all those perquisites of masculinity institutionalized within the "old Patriarchal system," including a certain basic physical freedom, the power to defend oneself from abuse. Lacking such "authority," Clarissa is made to enact the fantasies of her persecutor, his endlessly obsessive, endlessly destructive fiction of her nature. Her experience finally is a paradigm of oppression: subject first to the debasing conceptualizations of others—above all the tyranny of a sexual ideology that inscribes the female body itself—she is made to submit ultimately to the physical violence that implicitly underpins this ideology. The relation between "Male-Delinquent" Lovelace and his "bauble" Clarissa replicates the classic division Frantz Fanon, in *The Wretched of the Earth*, saw between colonizer and colonized: "This world cut in two is inhabited by two different species," of which the former, "the agents of government," "speak the language of pure force."[10] With the act of rape Lovelace speaks such a language.

Clarissa's response is of a piece with that of the political victim: self-condemnation, demoralization, vast *anomie* of the spirit. Lacking consciousness of the sources of her suffering, she internalizes guilt. After the rape she accuses herself violently—most poignantly, for the original wish for discourse itself. "My crime," she writes, "was the corresponding with [Lovelace] at first, when prohibited so to do by those who had a right to my obedience" (vi, 138). Her long and weirdly complicated dying may be thought of as a curving movement, a swerve, out of the realm of human interpretation into silence. Clarissa foregoes discourse—and by extension leaves behind the world of reading. She will no longer seek out significance in the deceitful "Book of Nature." She chooses instead a kind of autism, indistinguishable finally from death itself. Gradually Clarissa enters that state which Weil describes as the lot of "those who have suffered too many blows"—the condition in which "that place in the heart from which the infliction of evil evokes a cry of surprise may seem to be dead. But it is never quite dead; it is simply unable to cry out any more. It has sunk into a state of dumb and ceaseless lamentation."[11] As the heroine ceases to cry out, and hence exits from the world of reading, the fiction bearing her name also begins to shut down.

In the last part of this book I turn to what this exemplary

10. Frantz Fanon, *The Wretched of the Earth*, trans. Constance Farrington (New York: Grove Press, 1963), p. 38.
11. Weil, "Human Personality," p. 316.

drama may imply for *us*—witnesses to the great hermeneutic *débâcle* played out in the fictional world, *Clarissa*'s real readers. What do the internal dynamics of "construction" and "force" suggest about our own reading? Clarissa's "Story" is what never really gets told in *Clarissa;* it is that text which is always interrupted, suspended, fragmented by the texts of others. That which we might at first assume to be her "Story"—the vast collection of letters, the fiction itself—is obviously no story in any conventional sense. Rather, it is a contradictory, roiling, multivocal system: more a concatenation of possible narratives told by different tellers, of whom the heroine is only one. The multiple-correspondent epistolary text is not a simple discourse—never, as Richardson himself held it to be, the transparent "History of a Young Lady," but a congeries, a cluster of disparate discourses.

This conflict of discourses embodied by the text complicates the reader's role in several ways. The pressure of multiple constructions within *Clarissa* enforces on us, first of all, a pervasive sense of the subjective nature of *meaning* itself—both with regard to the text and to the world. By proposing alternate accounts of the same putatively "real" phenomena, *Clarissa* constantly shifts attention away from the phenomena to the account-making process, to the way readers organize significance. As Ian Watt was one of the first to note, by its very diffuseness *Clarissa* impels its reader toward a revolutionary epistemology: a view that Nature, truth, indeed the "real" itself, exist first as private constructs, functions of subjective determination.[12] Within the fictional world "reality" is continuously inscribed and reinscribed by individual interpreters. Confronting this dissolution of *claritas*, the replacement of a single so-called objective narrative by a multiplicity of *interpretative* events, we are made conscious in turn of our own subjectivity, the arbitrariness of the ways we try to make

12. Ian Watt, *The Rise of the Novel* (Berkeley: University of California Press, 1957), chap. 6, "Private Experience and the Novel."

27

sense out of contradictory accounts—in short, of what Barthes has called the *productive* nature of our reading.

Clarissa's thematicization of interpretation is not without other implications, however. Because of the intricate fashion in which the fiction formalizes the hermeneutic conflict between the heroine and her persecutor—above all, because it equates the triumph of "artful" Lovelace's constructions over Clarissa's with his ultimate sexual triumph over her—it hints at a politics of criticism. Clarissa's sacrificial relation to Lovelacean "force" raises a certain inescapable question about our own meaning-making activities. What ideologies, what desires, what hidden relations of "force," condition the way we, as individual readers, make sense out of *Clarissa?* Given the mysterious and sensational nature of the text, whose account of things do we tend to favor? Most important, perhaps, whose letters—Clarissa's or Lovelace's—do we read sympathetically, and on what grounds? The fiction raises an obvious question, for instance, having to do with the relation between reading and sexuality: *Clarissa* tends, often in very subtle ways, to polarize male and female readers. This is part of its continuing interest; by taking sexual violence as its central action, it encourages us to examine the ways in which the gender of the reader (along with resulting differences of socialization and *power*) may condition those meanings he or she finds in the text. Do male and female readers respond differently to the "black transaction" at the heart of the text? My suspicion is that they do, at least initially. I have been concerned here, tangentially, to see whether or not *Clarissa*'s male critics have in fact tended to give implicitly "Lovelacean" casts to their readings—either consciously or unconsciously undermining the heroine's point of view and elevating that of her pursuer. I have likewise been interested to discover if an explicitly feminist reversal of such a tendency is possible.

Clarissa has implications finally, I would claim, which are nothing other than moral—but not in any vulgar didactic sense. Contrary to Richardson's own expectations, the novel's moral impact lies not in any simple programmatic "message"; the text is, after all, a plethora of contradictory messages. Rather, the moral dimension of *Clarissa* shows up in the way it compels a certain readerly self-examination. By tracing so searchingly the patterns of abuse and exploitation which occur when meanings are routinely and arbitrarily inscribed and reinscribed by interpreters, it invites us to examine the grounds of our own hermeneutic activity. Granting the reader recognition—through what one could call the *cathartic* moment of Clarissa's death—of the "constructive" (and potentially *de*structive) nature of the meanings he or she lives by, *Clarissa* opens up a space for judgment. It returns us to the matter of human suffering—the pain expressed by Clarissa in that line with which we began, the pain of being made a "cypher." Which human constructs exploit, turn others to mere "cyphers"? Which indeed, like Lovelace's "Rake's Creed," are grounded in tyrannical desires? By raising such questions, *Clarissa* allows for a mode of ethical self-consciousness. The fiction dramatizes, remarkably, a subtle argument about the troubling, intricate relations between semantic "constructions" and human "force." But it leaves to its reader the task of judging the relation of these operations, in turn, to human pain.

In approaching *Clarissa* and its ciphers, I have been less concerned than some with possible authorial dimensions to the text, and deal only briefly with the fascinating issue of Richardson's own wishes regarding readerly interpretation of his seductive "History." Twentieth-century criticism of *Clarissa* has in large part bound itself to matters of authorial intention—what Richardson *meant* to convey by his richly perverse text, the precise nature of his didactic concerns, what one might call archaeological dimensions of the fiction: its relation to the moral, social, and theological thought of its age. From the point of view of literary history, this recovery of

Clarissa's biographical and sociohistorical context has been invaluable. Every Richardsonian owes a great debt to the classic studies of A. D. McKillop, William Sale, and Ian Watt. Similarly, more recent scholarship by T. C. Duncan Eaves and Ben D. Kimpel, Doody and Kinkead-Weekes, Cynthia Griffin Wolff, and William B. Warner, among others, has clarified further what we know of Richardson, his beliefs and compulsions, and the complicated compositional history of the triumphant imaginative fiction he produced.[13]

My own interest, however, lies not so much with any voice of the author speaking through the text, as with the many voices of *reading* that *Clarissa* activates. I have tried to delineate at once the epistemological and ideological complexities of this multivocality. In attempting such description, I have drawn on several aspects of contemporary critical theory. Regarding the all-important matter of "construction" in the novel—and the fictional exposure of interpretation as an active process—I have benefited obviously from the recent proliferation of reader-oriented approaches to narrative: the writings, for example, of the late Roland Barthes, Tzvetan Todorov, Paul de Man, Wolfgang Iser, and Stanley Fish. Barthes's *S/Z* in particular has been of much relevance here. His virtuoso demonstration of a new critical practice—in which the critic sets out not to espouse a single reading of a text but to indicate how various readers *might* read it, to show, in effect, what desires, ideological constraints, and structures of power inform interpretation—has influenced my own "deconstruction" of the dynamics of reading within and without *Clarissa*. At the same time, however, in an effort to link the hermeneutic question to the issue of power relations in the fictional world and show that Clarissa's experience has a politicosexual aspect, I have drawn on recent feminist critiques of the novel. Essays by Nancy K. Miller, Janet

13. For a summary of recent Richardson scholarship see Bibliographic Postscript.

Introduction

Todd, and Rachel Brownstein have been helpful in sorting out the sexual dimensions of "authority" within the fiction. More generally, recent feminist writing on the subject of women's speech and the constraints that historically have limited the power of women to articulate freely has influenced my account of the various "interruptions," literal and otherwise, Clarissa is made to suffer. Tillie Olsen's *Silences*, Michelle Cliff's essay "The Resonance of Interruption," and Adrienne Rich's writings in *On Lies, Secrets, and Silence* turn attention to the relation between the "interruption," censoring, and self-censoring of female discourse and the larger pattern of women's oppression. These authors have been concerned with the internal and external situations that have kept women from telling their own "stories." Cliff's remarks in particular, I think, have an unmistakable resonance for the feminist reader of *Clarissa:* "If we multiply one woman's silence of self across space and over time, we may see that the cultural history of women takes the form of an interrupted sequence of silences: outright silence, the inability to speak; or silence about the self, the inability to reveal." Interruptions and silences (including self-imposed silences such as Clarissa's ultimate rejection of language) result, most profoundly, from "violent invasions—invasions of the self, invasions of the group."[14]

I consider the book that follows more an experiment in criticism, finally, than a reading in the conventional sense. Regarding the interpretative choices I have made, I can only hope, with Clarissa, that the reader will put the best and not the worst construction on what it is I do.

14. Cliff, p. 35. See also Nancy K. Miller, *The Heroine's Text: Readings in the French and English Novel 1722–1782* (New York: Columbia University Press, 1980); Janet Todd, *Women's Friendship in Literature* (New York: Columbia University Press, 1980); and Rachel Mayer Brownstein, '"An Exemplar to Her Sex"': Richardson's Clarissa," *Yale Review*, 67 (1977), 30–47. For feminist treatments of women's relations to language generally see, besides Cliff's essay, Tillie Olsen's *Silences* (New York: Dell, 1978), and Adrienne Rich's collection of essays *On Lies, Secrets, and Silence: Selected Prose 1966–1978* (New York: Norton, 1979).

Clarissa by Halves

Even in death Clarissa Harlowe is broken in upon, ravaged—her story cut in half. Into the midst of Belford's reverent account of her posthumous affairs, a gross and delirious scenario intrudes—the bloated, kitschy death of her former tormentor, Mrs. Sinclair. The scene of the infamous "Mother's" demise, one of Richardson's more tumid Gothic spectacles, fractures Clarissa's own pious "History." It shatters the precarious narrative calm, the illusion of closure, marked off by the heroine's own holy dying. Clarissa's peace, and the peace of the text, is breached—snapped in two—by this final outrageous interruption. For the reader too, the sense of violation is extreme: the decorum, the funereal complacency of our reading is also breached. The flow of empathy—toward Clarissa, all in white—is rudely diverted, docked, by the interjection of grotesquerie.

Perversely, the intruding episode is itself concerned, on a number of levels, with rupture. It is an allegory of broken surfaces and amputations, of halvings of all kinds. The description, from Belford's pen, of the harlot's deathbed obsessively draws a world of interruption, split forms and partial objects. Mrs. Sinclair, we recall, dies of a leg "fracture" that she has received falling on the stairway connecting the two halves of her evil split-level house. When Belford, leaving behind Clarissa's affairs, arrives at the brothel to witness Sinclair's grisly end, the mortification has spread "half-way of the *Femur.*" The attending surgeons, barbarously gleeful, are ready to "*whip off her leg in a moment*" (VIII, 62). The screaming Sinclair, not surprisingly, has to be held down—by "half a dozen" harlots—"Harpyes"—half-women, half-monsters, in "shocking dishabille." The bodies of these attendants are motley, discontinuous visual forms:

> with faces, three or four of them, that had run, the paint lying in streaky seams not half blowz'd off, discovering coarse wrinkled skins: The hair of some of them of divers colours, obliged to the black-lead comb where black was affected: the artificial jet, however, yielding apace to the natural brindle: That of others plastered with oil and powder; the oil predominating: But every one's hanging about her ears and neck in broken curls, or ragged ends. [VIII, 55]

Belford's primary imagery here of broken surfaces, streaking, of chaotic division (he returns again to the "plastering fucus" on the prostitutes' faces, and their eyes, "half-opened, winking and pinking"), carries over into his description of Sinclair's own body, spread, in all its massiveness and corruption, on the tumbled bed. Her "clouted head dress being half off," Sinclair thrashes convulsively, orgasmically—"her wide mouth, by reason of the contraction of her forehead (which seemed to be half-lost in its own frightful furrows) splitting her face, as it were, into two parts" (VIII, 57). While her hands clench and unclench in agony, her "various-coloured breasts" heave "by turns." The effect of discontinuity and manic alternation is finally vocal as well as visual. Sinclair's attempts at coherent speech are violently "interrupted by groans"—"No time to repent!—And in a few hours (Oh!—Oh!—with another long howling O—h! U—gh—o! a kind of screaming key terminat-

ing it)" (VIII, 58)—and break off at last in "an inarticulate
frightful howl" that leaves everyone else "half-frighted." Her
last garbled shout suggests the breaking off, by death, of life
itself—"What—die! What! cut off in the midst of my sins!"
(VIII, 65).

Belford writes to Lovelace that his purpose in drawing out
the grotesque spectacular of Sinclair's death (even while mad-
dened Lovelace clutches at information about the other dead
woman, Clarissa) is to see if he can shock him "but half as
much" with his description "as I was shocked by what I saw
and heard" (VIII, 60). The final irony, however, is that Belford's own account of the horrible event is, like everything else
here, "cut off" in the midst. Anxiety, brought on by the scene
he has witnessed, forces him to drop his "trembling pen." An
anonymous, italicized, censoring voice (Richardson the
editor?) suggests that we "have done" with so "shocking" a
subject, "at once."

But can we? The text returns to Clarissa's drawn-out ob-
sequies, but the great tableau of Sinclair's dissolution does not
disappear so easily. The harlot's mangled, hallucinatory car-
cass lingers, and intrudes upon the reader's view of the other
corpse, Clarissa's own. The relation between Mother
Sinclair's blithering, disgusting end and the heroine's "bless-
ed" demise is not just one of antitype either. Contrasting the
death scenes of the two women (Clarissa's has come earlier, at
the end of Volume VII), Margaret Doody has suggested that
Sinclair's raving death is meant as a demonic counterpoint to
the heroine's final Christian composure. "[Sinclair's] deathbed
scene is in grouping and detail an intentional contrast to the
deathbed of Clarissa: Clarissa, pale and fragile (as unlike the
fat flushed bawd as possible), lies in bed surrounded by a
carefully defined group of figures" whose orderly gestures
express "grief and piety."[1] Sinclair's cohorts, on the other

1. Margaret A. Doody, *A Natural Passion: A Study of the Novels of Samuel Richardson* (London: Oxford University Press at the Clarendon Press, 1974), p. 219.

hand, show only "fear and confusion." While what Doody says of the displacement of figures in the two scenes is true, on the more intimate level of the image such clear antinomies do not endure for long. In *Clarissa*, as in the syntax of dreams (where, as Freud saw, the "either/or" tends to become a "both/and"), apparent contraries merge, opposites meet halfway: Sinclair and Clarissa are not, in fact, as "unlike as possible."

The curious, troubling link between them is the motif of interrupted form. As numerous characters reiterate toward the end of the novel, dead Clarissa, victim of interference, has been "cut off" too soon, her will to live "broken." When her actual corpse is viewed, late in Volume vıı, a strange overlay with Mrs. Sinclair is visually rendered. Most shockingly, Clarissa, parodying her dead "Mother," appears now as a kind of half-woman. Like the woman sawed in two in the magician's trick, she too has become a split form. According to her wish her coffin lid is "half-screwed down," thus presenting a partial, or interrupted view of her corpse. Seeing (part of) Clarissa, Anna Howe cries to Morden, "You knew not the Excellence, no, not *half* the Excellence that is thus laid low!" (vıı, 87). On the coffin lid itself, Clarissa's emblem of halving—the device of the lily with its stem "snapt short off" near the bloom—links her again to the brothel keeper. Sinclair's mortal fracture, "high in her leg," is bathetically preserved in this icon (an upside-down L), as are traces of all the other splittings, breakages, and disruptions already seen.

In *Clarissa*, the woman's body (prototypically rendered in the dying Sinclair and repeated in the heroine's corpse) is broken, incomplete, motley—disturbingly discontinuous. This image of interrupted form, here the fantastical shape of the dead woman, has consequences for a reading of *Clarissa* in its entirety. I began this introduction by moving from an instance of fragmentation in our reading of the text of *Clarissa* (the anecdote of Sinclair's death *intrudes* somehow into a would-be orderly narrative sequence, the posthumous record of the heroine) to instances of fragmentation dramatized within the disruptive anecdote itself. We can now make the same move in reverse. If the body of the woman, suspended finally in death at the heart of the fiction, is a broken form, so too in some sense is the text of Richardson's great novel itself. Again, Anna—pointing to Clarissa in her coffin: "And is this All!—Is it All, of my CLARISSA's Story?... This cannot, surely, be All of my CLARISSA's Story!" (VIII, 86-87). Anna's phantasmic merging of the heroine's body with her mysterious "Story"—both, apparently, lacking some essential—is significant. If the actual view of Clarissa's body is here interrupted, so likewise is our view of her "Story." Indeed, what *is* it? Even after eight volumes, the reader of *Clarissa*, like Cousin Morden, does not, perhaps, see "half" her excellence. Her history has come to us in a narrative that, while huge to the point of indecorousness, seems also perpetually incomplete. Our sense of what has in fact happened is obscure. Anna's question is the reader's also: Is it all?

Monstrously distended, Richardson's fiction of letters is at the same time fractured. *Clarissa* is split into pieces—the hundreds of letters of different correspondents—letters that are in turn fragmented by internal oddities: typographic changes, editorial "extractions," abrupt ellipses, hints of forgery. This fracturing makes for a basic problem of reading. At all points in the text one confronts marks of formal indeterminacy— letters interrupt (and contradict) others, vital information is omitted. Those elements of significance readers normally search for in fiction (transparent cause-effect relations, the resolution of ambiguities—indeed, all the features of a clearly realized plot) are either lacking, or mysteriously inconclusive. Paradoxically, the more we read in the matter of *Clarissa*, the less we may feel we know of the heroine. She lies at the center of the fiction—a woman broken in upon by rape, by death— and the shape of her "Story" repeats the signs of violation, by gaps in its linguistic surface, and in its structure of meaning.

Clarissa by Halves

Across the vast and peculiar narrative that bears her name, the truth about the heroine's history does not accumulate, but seems perpetually halved, disrupted, thrown into question. But here we come back upon Sinclair, and the garishness of her form. Intruding into the last solemn volume of Clarissa's dismal history, Sinclair's "huge, quaggy carcase" (*quaggy* = boggy, yielding, too soft to sustain weight) is a great summarizing image of Richardson's own problematic text. Her body is a message about discontinuity, and it signals, on a hallucinatory plane, the discontinuity of *Clarissa* itself. Confronting her jarring, phantasmic form, spread out in death, the reader is reminded of the corrupted surface, the frantic dissolves, of Richardson's "quaggy" narrative. The image of the marred, partial female form is an image of the "Story" that does not get fully told but is everywhere dislocated. Like Mother Sinclair Clarissa Harlowe is a fallen woman, and one "broken" by her fall. But one might say also that *Clarissa Harlowe* is a fallen text. It exposes on all levels the interruption, the disordering, of signification. It is hard to read.

2

Discovering Reading

The problem of "Story" is always at hand in *Clarissa*. What—where—is Clarissa's "Story"—the one Anna Howe, in her first letter to the heroine, "longs to hear"? Again, entering Richardson's lurching, exhausting text, with its mysterious lesions and effusions, its layerings of deceit and disclosure, one is never sure. Is it that "strange melancholy accident" to which all the babbling voices of the text seem to allude—the heroine's murky passage through abduction, rape, and death? Or is it in some sense the text itself—the "novel in letters," this artificial collation of disparate utterances, all ostensibly speaking of her? If it is in fact the latter, how are we intended to make sense out of it? The issue here—which is indeed the issue of reading—is raised, of course, in a number of eighteenth-century works that share a similarly elusive relation to "Story." *A Tale of a Tub, Roxana, Tristram Shandy*, and (crossing over into the realm of visual representation) the Hogarthian progresses come to mind. In each of these works, a radical ambiguity at the heart of the narrative invites us to wonder what the work is in fact meant to be *about*, what the nature of the communication we are being offered is. In Richardson's novel, however, the problem is given a tragic controlling insistence, an emotional extension, which we do not find elsewhere. The ambiguities attached to Clarissa's "Story" have implications for the reader which are unmatched in eighteenth-century literature—even, one must say, by those bleak and sad moments in *Tristram Shandy* when Tristram, caught in the mystery of language itself, seems to perform a dance of death with his own text. To read *Clarissa* is in some sense to become involved in a fundamentally anxious process: the search for "Story" engages the reader, like the heroine, in a confrontation with that which is not clear, a world of dim, flitting forms, only "faintly and imperfectly" seen.

Since its publication, commentators on *Clarissa* (including, as we will see, Richardson himself) have sought to cope with the overwhelming nature of the fiction by delimiting its "Story"—its range of possible meaning—in various ways. In this century alone, since the renewal of critical interest in Richardson following on the pioneering work of William Sale, A. D. McKillop, and Ian Watt, the novel has been subject to wildly differing interpretations. Classically, modern readers find in Richardson's text statements of one kind or another. Thus *Clarissa* has been seen, variously, as commentary on the perversion of parental authority, as Christian paradigm, as revelation of bourgeois social values and eighteenth-century class structure, as sexual myth (eliding at times into soft-core pornography), and most recently, as both feminist and antifeminist document.[1] Each of these readings, typically, has tended to exclude others, to highlight a certain content at the expense of other potential meanings. A look at the critical writing on *Clarissa* reveals an array of curiously blinkered versions of the text. Within individual interpretations, the blinkering effect can most often be seen, of course, in the treatment accorded the heroine herself—at times ecstatically

1. For a discussion of the sorts of symbolic "constructions" *Clarissa* has inspired, see Bibliographic Postscript.

laudatory, at times rabidly cynical. Critics who view her as a definitive moral center in the book, for instance, have often slighted the evidence for her psychological implication in her own "accident." Likewise, those who suggest her subliminal interest in the compromising situations leading up to the rape have underplayed, distressingly, the political dimensions of that act, and the radical misogyny of Lovelace's ultimate violence against her.

The fact that the plurality of readings assigned to Richardson's fiction have seldom cohered, one with another, and are often themselves troubled by questions of internal coherence, suggests at the start a basic difficulty adhering to the notion of meaning in *Clarissa*.[2] The image of discontinuity with which we began—the body of Mrs. Sinclair—pointed to a correspondence between phantasmic elements in the novel, an imagistic pattern, and what one might call the formal aspect of the text, the shape of narrative itself. The implication was that the phantasmic ultimately coincides with the epistemological—that hermeneutic ambiguity, the interruption, rather than the fulfillment of meaning and form, may in fact be what the fiction is all *about*. Indeed, the very multiplicity (and irreconcilability) of interpretation surrounding the text reaffirms the suspicion: *Clarissa* offers no "Story" in any conventional sense, but is concerned, on some level, with a problematization of the very notion of "Story" itself. More than has been previously acknowledged, *Clarissa*, like *Tristram Shandy*, is a fiction that investigates fiction making. It is a narrative concerned with the nature of meaning—how it is produced, how it is frustrated. This is another way of saying that it engages us, from the outset, in a crisis of reading.

The investigation of meaning in *Clarissa* is two-dimensional.

2. See William Beatty Warner's article "Proposal and Habitation: The Temporality and Authority of Interpretation in and about a Scene of Richardson's *Clarissa*," *boundary 2*, 7 (1979), 169-99, as well as *Reading Clarissa: The Struggles of Interpretation* (New Haven: Yale University Press, 1979).

Writing on narrative, the French linguist Emile Benveniste has distinguished between "two distinct and complementary systems" found in fiction: "story" (*histoire*) and "discourse" (*discours*).[3] The distinction here is between the history, or plot, that a narrative "tells," and the manner of presentation, its formal rhetoric. The same story, obviously, can be presented in different ways, using different kinds of discourse. In *Clarissa*, an elaboration of the problem of signification occurs in both systems simultaneously. Story and discourse (to follow Benveniste) both reflect upon a hermeneutic issue; both the plot and the rhetoric of the fiction introduce the question of meaning. Characters within the fiction—most powerfully, Clarissa herself—are caught up in various dilemmas of interpretation, yet so too is the reader "outside." The discontinuous, problematic form is simultaneously dramatized within (paradigmatically by the body of Sinclair), and modeled without (in the shape of the text we read).

It is necessary to make this initial separation between dimensions of the novel because, at the start, the very nature of *Clarissa*—epistolary in mode—tends to confuse them in our minds. At first glance, the classic novel in letters (with multiple correspondents) seems to merge *histoire* and *discours* in a peculiar manner. There is, of course, no conventional storyteller, no identifiable single voice of narration, intimated in the text. The narrative situation is radically unlike that in the familiar third-person novel, where, as Wayne Booth has shown, the reader is offered an image of an authorial *persona* (pointing back ultimately to the "implied author," that "second self" or "highly refined and selected version" of the real author) who tends to direct our reading process.[4] In *Emma*, thus, one is given traces of a narrative voice ("Austen"), and

3. Emile Benveniste, *Problèmes de linguistique générale* (Paris: Gallimard, 1966), p. 238; cited in Jonathan Culler, *Structuralist Poetics* (Ithaca: Cornell University Press, 1975), p. 197.

4. Wayne Booth, *The Rhetoric of Fiction* (Chicago: University of Chicago Press, 1961), p. 151.

comes to trust its perspective on the "story" being told. The reader can separate out the features of the rhetorical *persona* from the plot: *histoire* and *discours* appear distinguishable. In the epistolary form, however, narrative is not constructed around the simple fiction of a storyteller telling us a tale. Rather, it is composed of an odd assortment of imaginary, secondary *texts*—ostensibly produced by "characters," and out of which the reader (like a historian arranging documentary sources) must piece together a sequence of actions. The form itself, the collection of "letters," is the only "story" we are given. And the teller has disappeared altogether.

Despite the additional complexities posed by this situation, it is still possible to separate story and discourse, tale and presentation—at least for purposes of analysis. The key is the reading process, which in *Clarissa*, as in every piece of epistolary fiction, is itself two-dimensional. In a recent study of Choderlos de Laclos's *Les Liaisons dangereuses*, Ronald Rosbottom has described the bipartite reading process operating in the novel in letters. Laclos's novel—so much influenced by Richardson's—is likewise profoundly concerned with hermeneutics. It is *about* signification, "how things mean" (or fail to mean).[5] For Rosbottom, *Les Liaisons* does not contain a story in the conventional sense, but is rather an investigation of the processes of language. These processes, as the intricacies of the fiction demonstrate, are fundamentally unstable: *Les Liaisons* is, paradoxically, a message about the failure of messages to get across, about the failure of language (represented by the letter) to mediate between persons. It exposes "a perception of the insufficiency, on an ethical and aesthetic plane, of communicational codes in a highly developed culture."[6]

At the heart of Rosbottom's analysis is the epistolary form itself, and what he calls its all-important "thematicization" of

5. Ronald C. Rosbottom, *Choderlos de Laclos* (Boston: Twayne, 1978), p. 113.

6. Rosbottom, p. 101.

reading.[7] Always, at any moment in the novel in letters, two reading processes are going on: the reading within the fiction (that engaged in by the characters, the fictional senders and receivers) and the reading without (that of the real reader, you and me). The effect is of a hermeneutic overlay, or palimpsest. Our reading always follows, in some sense, another reading, another process of interpretation—that which we see dramatized in the fiction. Applying Benveniste's original distinction to the special case of the epistolary novel, the act of reading "built in" within the fiction might be identified with *histoire*, and our own reading process with *discours*. The internal drama of reading is, in effect, the primary "story" that the novel in letters unfolds; whereas our reading of the text recapitulates, on the formal plane, the fictionalized process of interpretation. Rosbottom writes: "We, the real readers, from our 'privileged' and artificially neutral status, are asked to structure the apparent disorder of an epistolary novel, thereby imitating the fictional readers who also are trying to order their responses to the stimuli of separate and contradictory letters."[8]

Yet this very palimpsest effect, as it heightens our consciousness of the reading process, brings us back upon the question of meaning. In the epistolary form, characteristically, the act of seeking meaning—interpretation itself—is repeatedly exposed as a problem-filled, perversely unconstrained, even hazardous occupation.

In both Richardson and Laclos, those very letters which make up the texts we read introduce the interpretative difficulty in its basic form. They are distressingly ambiguous linguistic artifacts: they symbolize communication, but do not necessarily embody it. Letters open themselves, promis-

---

7. In this, Rosbottom's analysis, as he acknowledges, draws much on the work of Todorov, specifically *Littérature et signification* (Paris: Larousse, 1967), pp. 39-49, and "The Discovery of Language: *Les Liaisons dangereuses* and *Adolphe*," *Yale French Studies*, 45 (1970), 113-26.

8. Rosbottom, p. 89.

cuously, to distortion by readers, who, out of naiveté or unscrupulousness, disregard the intended meaning of the letter writer. As we witness characters in epistolary novels responding (through subsequent replies or related correspondence) to letters they have received, we see also the degree to which they are able to misinterpret what they have read. Much of the often painful tension, as well as the irony, of both *Les Liaisons dangereuses* and *Clarissa* extends precisely out of the fact that we can compare actual letters with the fictional readers' interpretations. Characters show themselves (and Lovelace is a classic, disturbing example) reading according to whim alone—often with disastrous or violent consequences.

One might be tempted to call this kind of exploitation misreading and leave it at that, but it does, in fact, suggest the deeper problem—a philosophical one—at the heart of the letter. A letter is a text, and any text, Jacques Derrida claims, is, phenomenologically considered, a sign of absence. Writing originates out of a lack of presence, a metaphysical interruption. In *Of Grammatology* Derrida has suggested that the text is always only a substitute, or trace of being, rather than being itself.[9] The letter, one could say, is a paradigmatic text in that it is motivated by a dramatized human absence, the physical remove of the letter writer. It comes into existence as a substitute for the body of the writer, who (obviously) is not with the reader. "Indeed I have no delight," Clarissa writes to Miss Howe, "as I have often told you, equal to that which I take in conversing with you—By *Letter*, when I cannot in *Person*" (1, 29). But this banal condition—this motivating absence—also imposes on the letter what might be called its fundamental hermeneutic instability. At the time of reading, the letter is in

9. Jacques Derrida, *Of Grammatology*, trans. Gayatri Chakravorty Spivak (Baltimore: The Johns Hopkins University Press, 1974). See particularly Part I, "Writing before the Letter." See also Rosbottom's discussion of absence and presence in the epistolary novel, pp. 72–75.

some sense already a denatured artifact, cut off from its source in human presence. It is susceptible, hence, to the kind of indeterminacy that Derrida has shown to afflict all forms of writing: estrangement from "natural" significance, from a "human" point of origin. Meaning in the absolute sense (conventionally identified with the author's presence in a text, or authorial intention) is technically not available *in* the writing, which is always only a mark of absence. The message one extracts from the letter remains perpetually unverifiable. It cannot be referred back to human presence, to the writer.

But when the letter is viewed in this way, our sense of the nature of reading is also altered. Interpretation is revealed as an essentially arbitrary activity. Because of its denatured status, the letter opens itself (to use Clarissa's term) to any "construction" the reader may wish to impose. The appalling physical malleability of the letter—its vulnerability to deformation and change during transmission—is a sign of its hermeneutic instability. One never knows whether that which one reads is in fact the same document, physically speaking, as that which the writer sent. The linguistic artifact does not necessarily yield meaning; rather, meanings are generated, arbitrarily, by different readers. Readers interpret—as Rosbottom suggests in his description of the correspondence of Merteuil and Valmont in *Les Liaisons*—according only, finally, to the shape of their desire. Meaning is not so much retrieved from the letter—which is always an indeterminate linguistic structure—as projected onto it. And these projections are multiple, just as the operations of desire themselves are multiple. Every reading thus becomes in some sense a misreading, in that it is an imposition on the text, and may or may not coincide with the writer's intended meaning.

This process of projection is what we, the real readers, see going on, of course, inside the novel in letters. Yet as we do so, we are forced to confront the problematics of our own reading. What are the constraints, if any, on our own interpretative acts? To what extent is our sense of "what happens" in the fictional world a "construction"? The last question is central to *Clarissa*. As we consider the way in which characters draw meaning from the letters they read, we must likewise consider the way in which we assign significance—to the fiction itself. John Preston is right when, in an elegant essay on the role of the reader in *Clarissa*, he describes the initial peculiarity of Richardson's epistolary situation—"The actual process of writing, the text itself, is the action. It is not a description or narration of the action, though it contains many such descriptions.... The words in the novel are the acts."[10] The only events in epistolary fiction, strictly speaking, are events of language. But one must add that these strange "acts," because they are in fact "words," point toward the issue of textual exegesis—and always, on two tiers. Inside Richardson's novel, the process of signification is no longer innocent; the desire of the reader is shown interrupting the ideal flow of meaning from writer's pen (an image of presence) to the world. Yet precisely because reading inside is dramatized as a compromised, and compromising, activity, the real reader's role is similarly exposed. In the remainder of this book, I shall be concerned with looking in more detail at this dynamic, first by examining the radical critique of interpretation suggested by Clarissa's own "Story"—the internal drama of reading—and then by showing how this critique impinges on the external drama, our relation to *Clarissa* itself. We cannot escape the implications, hermeneutic and moral, of the act of reading we witness: it reflects, always, our own.

10. John Preston, *The Created Self: The Role of the Reader in Eighteenth-Century Fiction* (London: Heinemann, 1970), p. 91.

3

Reading the Letter,
Reading the World

To speak of the image of reading dramatized inside
Richardson's novel is to speak from the start of a process more
complicated and far-reaching than the word "reading" usually
connotes. I have been using "reading" interchangeably with
"exegesis" and "interpretation"—to suggest an activity: reading as a kind of *work*, or operation. *Clarissa* enforces such an
identification. The active deciphering of texts is the work in
which all the characters are engaged. (We will examine the
corollary activity—writing—shortly.) Reading is their obsession, their joy and bewilderment. But this primary process of
interpretation points immediately to another: the interpretation of experience itself. Reading carries an existential force in
Clarissa. Most fully conceived, it is that act through which
individuals constitute themselves, and define their connec-
tions with the world of other people.

In the most basic sense, existence in the fictional world
depends on reading. To be *in* an epistolary novel at all, one
has to be a reader. Clarissa, Lovelace, Anna, Belford, and the
rest exist for us as characters in that each is first of all a reader,
a participant in that system of linguistic exchange—the great
"Series of Letters" which gives rise to the text. Entry into the

world of the letter, the world of signifying systems, is the necessary condition for fictional *life*. The self is defined through its relation to the social realm, represented here by language. A parallel can be drawn between this situation and the one Tzvetan Todorov has seen operating in story collections such as *The Thousand and One Nights*. There, according to Todorov, "the only constant of the psychology of the characters (or of the psychological presuppositions on which the work is founded) lies in the obsession with telling and listening to stories: what defines a character as a compositional unit is the fact of having a story to tell, and from the point of view of their ultimate destinies, 'narration equals life; the absence of narration, death.'"[1] Clarissa "lives"—that is, exists as what Todorov has termed a "compositional unit"—to the extent that she attempts to interpret, to the extent that she becomes visible to us as the recipient and reader of texts.

It may be objected (particularly in view of Todorov's remarks, which emphasize the creation of "narrative" over reading per se) that I am ignoring a more obvious activity characters in the novel perform—writing. Are not, one might ask, Clarissa and Lovelace defined as writers as much as readers? Can we not in fact describe them as first producers, rather than interpreters, of letters? In the more expansive, indeed existential model of reading I am suggesting, however, writing falls into place. Writing is a necessary corollary of reading, but reading remains, phenomenologically speaking, primary.

Everywhere in *Clarissa*, first of all, the act of reading is a paradigm for the way in which characters interpret the world. They read in the literal sense; yet this activity modulates, metaphorically, into another sort of cognitive operation: their ongoing attempt to order events, to make sense out of what is happening to them. All the major correspondents in *Clarissa*

1. Tzvetan Todorov, *Grammaire du Decameron* (The Hague: Mouton, 1969), p. 92; cited by Fredric Jameson in *The Prison-House of Language* (Princeton: Princeton University Press, 1972), p. 199.

are conscious of themselves as readers in this larger sense; characteristically, they like to confuse the textual and the experiential in their own discourse. They tend to speak of themselves (and others) as *texts*. (From indications in his correspondence—particularly the letters to Lady Bradshaigh—Richardson himself seems to have been afflicted with the same confusion.[2]) Like medieval rhetoricians, Clarissa, Lovelace, and the rest are absorbed in a vision of the world itself as Book, open to interpretation. Textual exegesis becomes for them the most obvious and congenial model for more expansive kinds of intellectual ordering. Thus Lovelace will refer at times to "the science of reading men," and crow, with typical hubris, how his skill at this kind of reading surpasses Belford's. In turn Clarissa speaks of herself, poignantly enough, as a sort of text, unfortunately open to the wild and unconstrained interpretations of others: "I am but a *cypher*, to give *him* significance and *myself* pain" (IV, 40). Objects and events in the fictional world seem to signify like written words; physical gestures, even a person's "Looks" can be read. Faces become, surreally, articulating surfaces, almost like pages of a book. (As the heroine writes of Lovelace: "*Such* a man to be haughty, to be imperious!—The lines of his own face at the same time condemning him . . . ! [I, 208]). Examples of similar metaphoric exchanges abound in *Clarissa*. To pass through the world of the fiction is to pass through a seemingly

2. Richardson and Lady Bradshaigh corresponded for some time before meeting face to face. See Eaves and Kimpel's account of the peculiar ambivalence they seem to have had about arranging a personal interview. Lady Bradshaigh described one proposed meeting between them as a way of turning "a certain imaginary scene into reality," yet the difficulties they had achieving this end suggest their unwillingness to let go of their "textual" preconceptions of each other. T. C. Duncan Eaves and Ben D. Kimpel, *Samuel Richardson: A Biography* (Oxford: Oxford University Press at the Clarendon Press, 1979), pp. 225–27. On Richardson's relationship with Lady Bradshaigh see also John Traugott, "*Clarissa*'s Richardson: An Essay to Find the Reader," in *English Literature in the Age of Disguise*, ed. Maximillian E. Novak (Berkeley: University of California Press, 1977).

legible field—one, like the letter itself, that opens itself everywhere to the reader's "construction."

And the place of writing in all of this? The basic cognitive activity that characters in *Clarissa* perform—reading their experience—motivates the epistolary world. It leads inexorably to articulation, and the production of real texts. The actual letter, one could say, is a reading taken of one's experience. Individuals confront and interpret events; the letter registers, or recapitulates this initial hermeneutic process. The letter is the visible trace left by a prior apprehension of the world; it is an attempt to preserve meaning. In *Hints of Prefaces for Clarissa*, Richardson, following Locke, makes the epistemological sequence explicit. The mind receives from without certain impressions, which it then orders and re-presents in language. Letters, he writes, are "the only natural Opportunity that could be had, of representing with any Grace those lively and delicate Impressions, which *Things present* are known to make upon the Minds of those affected by them."[3] The text one produces is technically a writing, but it is founded upon and reflects a more basic intellectual gesture, an act of reading the world of perception. (Critical discourse holds on to the same paradox, of course: one's interpretation of, say, a literary work, though written down, is still called a "reading" of the work.) In the epistolary novel, thus, writing is not an isolated activity, but is part of a larger hermeneutic circuit in which the characters are caught up.

The correspondents in *Clarissa* exist for us first, then, as readers of actual texts. This basic identity in turn suggests, metaphorically, their greater pursuit—the active deciphering of experience itself. They seek above all to decode their world; and their own letters (those "*instantaneous* Descriptions and

3. Richardson, *Hints of Prefaces for Clarissa*, in the Augustan Reprint Society edition of *Clarissa: Preface, Hints of Prefaces, and Postscript*, ed. R. F. Brissenden (Los Angeles: William Andrews Clark Memorial Library, 1964), p. 6.

Reflections" on "critical situations," in Richardson's words[4]) are the continuous record of this endeavor.

There is a problem in all of this, of course—and here we encounter the central catastrophe dramatized in *Clarissa*. The problem lies in an essential arbitrariness in the decoding act itself. In *S/Z* and elsewhere, Roland Barthes has posited the intrinsic subjectivity of textual exegesis. In the Barthesian formulation, meaning does not somehow lie *in* a text—in a narrative, for example—like ore awaiting excavation by a reader. The text is never a transparent container for a certain content. Owing to its status as a linguistic object, its nature is always polysemous. (In this respect it reminds us immediately of the letters that make up the epistolary world.) Thus, confronting the same textual material—which like any sign system is ultimately arbitrary in significance—readers organize it differently, according to their different psychological, social, and cultural expectations. Readers *produce* meaning for the text: out of many possibilities, a reader will construct one, around the text, so to speak. This act of production may proceed in accordance with basic conventions of reading, derived from exposure to other texts (in the case of narrative, thus: expectations about "plot," temporal sequence, "realistic" character portrayal, etc.); but the end result, the meaning one makes for the work, is idiosyncratic, the product of an essentially private contingency. "The goal of literary work (of literature as work)," Barthes proposes, "is to make the reader no longer a consumer, but a producer of the text."[5] In his paradoxical formulation (which again puts us in mind of the intricate relation in the novel in letters between reading, in the larger sense, and articulation), the reader *writes* the text. From the disarmingly elusive, multivalent literary object, we extract a model of significance (or try to). Barthes invokes the reader's

4. Preface, *Clarissa* (I, xiv).
5. Roland Barthes, *S/Z*, trans. Richard Miller (New York: Hill & Wang, 1974), p. 4.

interpretative freedom: as we interpret, we are in fact inscribing that text we experience. And thus it follows that there are,
finally, as many versions of this text as there are individual
readers and readings.

Contemporary hermeneutic theorists, including Barthes,
make the same metaphoric conflation that, as I have already
suggested, takes place in *Clarissa:* reading is a process
analogous, if not identical, to the way human beings make sense
of the world generally.[6] In essays in *Mythologies* and *Image—
Music—Text*, for instance, Barthes pointed up the relationship
between textual interpretation, considered as an act of production, and the way in which individuals form coherence out of
phenomenological events.[7] Human beings read cultural sign
systems in much the same fashion that readers read texts.
Jonathan Culler makes the same relation explicit in *Structuralist Poetics*. Speaking first of recent critical theory, he
writes: "Granting new attention to the activity of reading, it
would attempt to specify how we go about making sense of
texts, what are the interpretive operations on which literature
itself, as an institution, is based."[8] Yet to investigate reading in
a literary context is simultaneously to investigate "modes of
ordering" generally. Studying narrative, suggests Culler, ultimately enables a person "to understand how he [or she]
makes sense of the world."[9] "The novel is the primary semiotic agent of intelligibility" in Western culture. Hence, to examine how one produces meaning for it is to examine the
grounds of intelligibility itself.

6. See Jonathan Culler's bibliography of contemporary hermeneutic
theory in *Structuralist Poetics* (Ithaca: Cornell University Press, 1975), as
well as his general overview of recent theories of reading in Part II of the
same book, "Poetics."
7. See Barthes's "readings" of pop culture artifacts in the early collection
Mythologies, trans. Annette Lavers (London: Jonathan Cape, 1972) and most
recently in *The Eiffel Tower*, trans. Richard Howard (New York: Hill &
Wang, 1979).
8. Culler, p. viii.
9. Culler, p. 238.

Reading the Letter, Reading the World

If the analogy between the active model of reading and the way we look at the world holds good, however, the ontological implication is striking. One's reading of experience itself is also only an arbitrary "construction"—the product of an internal cognitive operation. If reading is creative, and we in some sense write into being the text we read, we also write into being the world we think we perceive. This discovery has been made in this century by cultural anthropologists: what is viewed as the orderly phenomenal world, they suggest, exists first always only as a construct, produced by individuals out of an indeterminate experiential flux. That which appears to be the nature of things is in fact an artificial representation, a human projection grounded in history and in culture. Hans Vaihinger proposes that human systems, all social and psychological modes of ordering, can be thought of as fictional structures, as "as if" constructions—no matter how natural they seem.[10] (Food taboos provide a classic illustration, for as any cross-cultural study shows, societies make different decisions about what is edible and what is not. Though the food taboo is perceived as coming from Nature, it models a cultural, rather than a natural category. It reflects a cultural interpretation of what Nature is.) Readers, the structuralists point out, tend to naturalize meaning in texts. That is, even though the reader produces meaning, actively, in the moment of reading, this significance seems to be immanent, to have been present in the text all along. In the same way, however, individuals naturalize the world of perception. We invest phenomena with significance, yet these projected meanings then appear to inhere in the phenomena themselves.

In the social realm, thus, the various sign systems that one encounters—spoken and written language, gestures, the etiquette system, clothing—seem to communicate naturally. Certain interpretations of phenomena, when validated by a

10. See Harold Toliver, *Animate Illusions: Explorations of Narrative Structure* (Lincoln: University of Nebraska Press, 1974), p. 39.

social group, become ideological, part of a larger collective "construction" of reality.[11] The apparent meaning we find in human behavior does not flow, however, from the nature of things, but results from arbitrary cultural (or, one could say, political) determinations. The flux of sensory phenomena seems to form significant patterns before our eyes; we detect signs of Nature in it—orderly, absolute, legible. But as Stanley Fish suggests, the category of the natural itself is "not essential but conventional." It refers "not to properties of the world but to properties of the world as it is given to us by our interpretive assumptions"—and is the result of a cognitive act "performed at so deep a level it is indistinguishable from consciousness itself."[12] The meaning we read in the world of phenomena, then, is always in some sense only that meaning we have made—a contingent, mutable, human meaning. Nothing we can know—apart from our own inventive capacity, and our own desire—"dictates" the way we decode (i.e., write) the text that is the world. In Lovelace's gleeful formula, the world one sees is always but a manifestation, finally, of "Art"—the shaping imagination itself.

In *Clarissa* this arbitrariness—the *license* at the heart of the interpretative act—makes for tragedy. The world its characters confront, first of all, is troublingly ambiguous. It is not a lucid text; what it signifies is neither fixed nor absolute. If interpretation of the letter is an unlimited, ultimately unstoppable process, interpretation of the world is likewise free of constraint. "Nature" does not condition meaning. Characters may speak of "Nature," identifying it with the truth and con-

11. Durkheimian social theory is organized around this point. For an overview of twentieth-century developments in the sociology of knowledge see Peter L. Berger and Thomas Luckmann, *The Social Construction of Reality* (New York: Doubleday, 1966).

12. Stanley Fish, "Normal Circumstances, Literal Language, Direct Speech Acts, the Ordinary, the Everyday, the Obvious, What Goes without Saying, and Other Special Cases," *Critical Inquiry*, 4 (1978), 626-27.

trasting it with "Art"—as in Clarissa's reading of Lovelace, "I see his gentleness was *Art:* Fierceness, and a temper... are *Nature* in him" (II, 129). But the "natural" has no binding or privileged force in the fictional world: it exists only as a linguistic construct, a counter in the speech of various characters. Its definition changes with context. Or rather, meaning is conditioned by individual acts of interpretative aggression. As Lovelace is so fond of pointing out, it is always possible to "turn *Black White*"—to say something is and have it so. Our conventional sense of reality itself tends to dissolve in the fictional world. At any given moment, the real is a function of personal vision; the world is an inscription, traced by the individual consciousness. A kind of hermeneutic *libertinage* prevails.

This phenomenological situation is not unlike that embraced by Henry James in *The Future of the Novel:*

> How childish... to believe in reality, since we each carry our own in our thought and in our organs. Our eyes, our ears, our sense of smell, of taste, differing from one person to another, create as many truths as there are men upon earth.... Each one of us, therefore, forms for himself an illusion of the world, which is the illusion poetic, or sentimental, or joyous, or melancholy, or unclean, or dismal, according to his nature. And the writer has no other mission than to reproduce faithfully this illusion, with all the contrivances of art that he has learned and has at his command. The illusion of beauty, which is a human convention: the illusion of ugliness, which is a changing opinion: the illusion of truth, which is never immutable.[13]

The crucial difference between the Richardsonian and Jamesian stance, however, is that whereas James shows a complacency, an almost Barthesian *plaisir*, in contemplating the ar-

13. Henry James, *The Future of the Novel*, ed. Leon Edel (New York: Random House, 1956), p. 196.

bitrariness of human constructs, Richardson weights the same situation with a tragic force. The freedom associated with interpretation leads in *Clarissa* to violence, exploitation, abuse. Because the world does not signify naturally, because one's reading is all, a ground for human conflict opens up. Characters in Richardson's novel collide in an effort to impose their "constructions" on others. They use various kinds of pressure (modulating into sexual violence, in the case of Lovelace and his "charmer dear") in the attempt to validate their versions of the real. As William Beatty Warner has remarked in *Reading Clarissa*, the letter is always a primary instrument in this "struggle of interpretations"; for the letter can be seen not just as an attempt to articulate, for oneself, a reading of experience, but as a mode of imposing this reading on the other—one's correspondent.[14] Interpretation is politicized. Meaning is legitimated finally by personal power alone, by one's ability to intimidate. The anarchy and aggression associated with reading thus breeds a kind of tragic violence. To see the human face of this tragedy in *Clarissa* we must turn at once to the heroine.

14. See Warner, "Subjecting the Reader to Personal Correspondence," in *Reading Clarissa: The Struggles of Interpretation* (New Haven: Yale University Press, 1979), p. 96.

4

Interrupting "Miss Clary"

Clarissa Harlowe's "harrowing tale" turns upon a confrontation with the arbitrariness of signs, with the failure of things to yield meaning, simply, absolutely. Her catastrophe is a catastrophe of reading. She does not understand either the complexity or the compromised nature of the process. And hence she is a victim—of her own reading, and the readings of others. She is caught up, one might say, in a pathology of reading.

In a famous passage early on, Anna Howe writes to Clarissa that "I am fitter for *this* world than you: You for the *next* than me" (1, 63). Part of Clarissa's uncanny quality lies in just this: while driven to seek out and participate in the human world, a world where meanings are read and articulated, she does not comprehend the pitfalls. Above all Richardson's heroine is a naive exegete. She reads the world as if it were an "open book"—a transparent source of meaning. Signs, she assumes, convey simple messages about Nature itself. Clarissa does not question the "signature" of the letter; she does not read between the lines. From the outset, those various codes of communication she tries to "penetrate"—the linguistic system, assorted visual and iconographic codes, the language of behavior—all seem to bespeak an objective order of things. For too long Clarissa remains unaware that the world of signs itself—like the letter—is multivalent; for too long she remains unaware that her own readings, not to mention those of others, are creative, artificial, idiosyncratic—grounded in desire. "How natural is it for people," her sister Bella rails at her, "when they set their hearts upon any-thing, to think everybody must see it with their eyes!" (I, 323). The politics of interpretation is unknown to her. For much of *Clarissa*, thus, the heroine travels blindly through the fictional landscape, without recognizing the true nature of that process which conditions the way she sees, and the way others see her. She holds, unconsciously, to a version of Addison's placid theorem of the meaningful: "It is but opening the eye, and the scene enters."

The agonizing and absurd abuse Clarissa is made to undergo, first at the hands of the Harlowes, then with Lovelace and his minions, involves a kind of continuous semiotic defamiliarization. Throughout her nightmarish experience, from house arrest at Harlowe-Place to rape and death, she is forced into confrontation with the ambiguity of human texts (both of the literal and metaphoric kind), and with the problematic nature of her own interpretative acts. Her sense of "Nature" is repeatedly disrupted, through a long process of humiliation, during which her ability to read what is going on around her is thwarted and parodied by others. Clarissa is tricked by actual letters, of course, which turn out to be forgeries, unnatural substitutes—but she is also tricked by the world of signs itself, which is equally denatured and open to manipulation by the unscrupulous. The violation she experiences is simultaneously a violation of her body and a violation of her sense of the meaningful. At the hands of Lovelace her body suffers a kind of interruption—marked out in the act of rape—but so too Clarissa is made to confront the interruption of that "natural" relation she assumes between text and meaning, the sign and reality. A gap is opened up in her vision of the world: sign and "Nature" split apart.

This dissolution of natural signification experienced by the heroine has a corollary, however. Discovering the arbitrariness of human constructs, she also discovers that her own readings have no privileged force. Her "construction" of events, even of the nature of her own desire, cannot contend with the brutal and devious readings of others—she is powerless against them and their implications. The odious "Hints" of others take on a controlling force in her life. Clarissa's progress through the fiction, like that of Hogarth's harlot, is a movement into increasingly incoherent systems; but it is also revelatory. She becomes conscious of interpretation itself as an act of "penetration"—an act of filling the gap left by the (incomplete) sign, an act of violence. And at that point, which is also the moment of death, she finds an escape—leaving behind the world of reading and the suffering it entails.

The shape of the hermeneutic disaster Clarissa is to undergo is set up from the start, in the first volumes of the novel. The scenes at Harlowe-Place, site of her first physical confinement, also establish the degree to which she is caught, suspended, in a consuming desire to *read*, to interpret and articulate her experience. Naively, she falls captive to what Ronald Rosbottom has called "the lure of meaning." Her family's persecutions prefigure those of Lovelace, and it is noteworthy that from the outset they are, in the profoundest sense, linguistic persecutions. The Harlowes play upon Clarissa's desire for simple meanings; they purposely confuse those codes of communication she is accustomed to use—both to signify her own experience and to interpret the behavior of others. As she attempts to make sense of their words and actions, indeed to converse with them, she is implicated in a dilemma of interpretation that intensifies across the fiction. They assault her skill as a reader, willfully, unremittingly.

The dispute between Clarissa and her family over whether

she will marry Solmes is couched always in terms of "authority"—the "tyrant word AUTHORITY," as Anna calls it. With its echo of a textual metaphor, the term defines the conflict as a linguistic one. (An elaborate play is made throughout *Clarissa* on authors and authority. The heroine's parents, embodiments of familial authority, are also the "authors" of her being, and become, in turn, the "authors of [her] persecution" [II, 266]. In time, of course, the latter epithet is transferred to Lovelace. Clarissa, in a sense, is being written and rewritten by everyone she encounters.) In a discussion of the *Odyssey*, Todorov has remarked that in the epic world "piety corresponds to silence; speech is linked to rebellion."[1] In the eyes of her family, Clarissa's attempts at articulation are in themselves, first of all, a basic sign of her revolt against their will. In the early parts of *Clarissa* there is much to suggest that the grotesque resentment of the heroine which surfaces among her relations is as much as anything a fear and envy of her remarkable powers of articulation. (What they really fear, of course, is the "construction," couched in language, which she might make of their own individious actions.) Since childhood, we learn, Clarissa has participated in the processes of language—speaking, reading, writing—with alacrity, and no apparent sense of the potential dangers. This history is alluded to by many correspondents in *Clarissa*, but we receive perhaps the most extensive account from Anna, retroactively, in Volume VIII. Speaking to Morden of Clarissa's youth, she describes how the heroine's fascination with language was marked out on all levels. "She was an admirable mistress," Anna writes, "of all the graces of elocution" (VIII, 223)—likewise, "the most graceful *Reader* I ever knew" (229). "Poetry was poetry indeed when she read it" (229). Her orthography, "even punctuation," was perfect, and she understood "the derivation as well as sense of the words she used, and . . . stopt

1. Tzvetan Todorov, *The Poetics of Prose*, trans. Richard Howard (Ithaca: Cornell University Press, 1977), p. 56.

not at *sound*, when she spelt accurately" (224). In addition to "critical knowledge of her own tongue," Clarissa had "an admirable facility in learning languages, and re'd with great ease both Italian and French" (225). Here and elsewhere, Clarissa's delight, above all, in writing itself is noted: her constant morning devotion, Anna writes, was always to her "epistolary amusements." The heroine is one, as her Uncle Antony points out, with an uncommon "knack" for "scribbling" (1, 234).

Clarissa has been defined historically, then, as a prodigy of language, a lively participant in the linguistic sign system. Yet there is a sense in which she has never known the risk she has taken. Again, Todorov: "to speak is to assume a responsibility, which is why it is also to incur a danger."[2] What Clarissa does not know yet is that by entering language itself she has entered a basic arena for human conflict; she has entered the primary realm in which "constructions" of experience collide. To articulate one's own reading is to risk being perceived by the other as an aggressor. Even in Anna's excessively laudatory account, it is intimated that Clarissa, by uttering her sense of things, has left those around her "speechless." She has taken language away from others, through sheer eloquence. "She had a talent of saying uncommon things in such an easy manner, that everybody thought they could have said the same; and which yet required both genius and observation to say them" (VIII, 230). This in itself is an ambiguous achievement, and in a family such as the Harlowes, one fraught with a certain peril.

When the family, led by James Harlowe and Arabella, come to persecute Clarissa—over the marriage issue, over her relation with Lovelace—her very "loquaciousness" emerges as a primary object of attack. What is really under attack, of course, is the heroine's capacity for reading, in the existential sense. The Harlowes abuse her for subverting their

2. Todorov, *Poetics of Prose*, p. 57.

"authority"—for challenging their collective interpretation of events, for challenging that vision of the world they have written into being. James, for example, taunts Clarissa specifically for being always a "ready scribbler" and equates her "whining vocatives" with her supposed iniquities (II, 30). Uncle Antony, as we have seen, speaks condescendingly and contemptuously of her "knack" of letter writing. Arabella makes perhaps the most vicious attack on Clarissa's eloquence when she accuses her of using her "silver tongue" to manipulate their grandfather before his death. As Clarissa recounts it in a letter to Anna, the attack begins in a general condemnation: "That I half-bewitched people by my insinuating address: That nobody could be valued or respected, but must stand like cyphers where-ever I came" (I, 316). But Arabella soon gets to the real point:

> Did you not bewitch my Grandfather? Could any-thing be pleasing to him, that *you* did not say or do? How did he use to hang, till he slabbered again, poor doting old man! on your silver tongue! Yet what did *you* say, that *we* could not have said? What did *you* do, that *we* did not endeavour to do? —And what was all this for? Why, truly, his Last Will shewed what effect your *smooth* obligingness had upon him! [I, 316–17]

Arabella's rhetoric here is a classic example of her own hermeneutic violence: it is Clarissa, ironically, who must "stand like a cypher" and be subject to Arabella's lurid reading of her behavior and her part in family history.

The linguistic oppression instituted by the Harlowes involves at the outset a number of crude attempts to "cut off," in the most literal way, Clarissa's ability to articulate. On the issue of the proposed alliance with Solmes, Clarissa's own words are disallowed—overtly, even physically. In conversation, she is broken in upon, "interrupted," even before she can speak.[3] Dialogue between the heroine and various members of her family is typically a discontinuous, jerky, one-sided affair. In an early altercation with her father, thus, Clarissa's own utterances are constantly halved by interruptions:

He turned from me, and in a strong voice, Clarissa Harlowe, said he, know, that I will be obeyed.

God forbid, Sir, that you should not!—I have never yet opposed your will—

Nor I your whimsies, Clarissa Harlowe, interrupted he. . . .

I was going to make protestations of duty—No protestations, girl! No words! I will not be prated to! I have no child, I *will* have no child, but an obedient one.

Sir, you never had reason, I hope—

Tell me not what I never *had*, but what I *have*, and what I *shall* have.

Good Sir, be pleased to hear me—My Brother and my Sister, I fear—

Your Brother and Sister shall not be spoken against, girl!—They have a just concern for the honour of my Family.

And I hope, Sir—

Hope nothing.—Tell me not of *hopes*, but of *facts*. I ask

3. Feminist linguists studying male/female conversation patterns suggest that male speakers have a greater tendency to interrupt female speakers than they do other male speakers, and that female speakers rarely interrupt male speakers. The willingness to let oneself be interrupted—as Clarissa is—may be part of what linguist Robin Lakoff calls "women's language," a set of speech habits, marked by hesitancy, indecisiveness, and insecurity, which women in male-dominated society typically develop, and which reflect their subservient place in that society. (Other characteristics of "women's speech" include the use of the tag question, polite forms, euphemism, and hyper-grammatical speech.) See Lakoff, *Language and Woman's Place* (New York: Harper & Row, 1975), and Casey Miller and Kate Swift, *Words and Women* (Garden City, N.Y.: Anchor Books, 1977), pp. 97-100. What looks like unbelievable deference in Clarissa may simply reflect her internalization of certain "feminine" speech patterns, and point again to her lack of power, within the patriarchal family unit and her society as a whole.

nothing of you but what is in your *power* to comply with, and what it is your *duty* to comply with.

Then, Sir, I *will* comply with it—But yet I hope from your goodness—

No expostulations! No *buts*, girl! No qualifyings! I will be obeyed, I tell you; and chearfully too!—or you are no child of mine!

I wept. [I, 52-53]

When Clarissa speaks with her mother, the same pattern of disruption is more subtle perhaps, yet equally pervasive. Mrs. Harlowe's interruptions become increasingly meaningless, and serve only to break the flow of her daughter's thought:

Were I to be Queen of the Universe [Clarissa begins], that dignity should not absolve me from my Duty to You, and to my Father. I would kneel for your blessings, were it in the presence of millions—So that—

I am loth to interrupt *you*, Clary; tho' you could more than once break in upon *me*. You are young and unbroken: But, with all this ostentation of your duty, I desire you to shew a little more deference to me when I am speaking.

I beg your pardon, dear Madam, and your patience with me on *such* an occasion as *this*. If I did not speak with earnestness upon it, I should be supposed to have only maidenly objections against a man I never can endure.

Clary Harlowe!—

Dearest, dearest Madam, permit me to speak what I have to say, this once—it is hard, it is *very* hard, to be forbidden to enter into the cause of all these misunderstandings, because I must not speak disrespectfully of one who supposes me in the way of his ambition, and treats me like a slave—

Whither, whither, Clary—

My dearest Mamma! —My duty will not permit me so far to suppose my Father arbitrary, as to make a plea of that arbitrariness to you—

How now, Clary!—O girl!

Clarissa herself is forced into more and more desperate statements, to no effect:

> Your patience, my dearest Mamma:—You were pleased to
> *say*, you would hear me with patience.—PERSON in a man is
> nothing, because I am supposed to be prudent: So my eye is to
> be disgusted, and my reason not convinced—
> Girl, girl! [I, 115-16]

At moments of the greatest violence (which unpleasantly
foreshadow scenes with Lovelace later), the Harlowes replace
simple vocal interruption with a kind of active physical suppression. As Clarissa tries to explain her feeling about Solmes,
her speech is literally blocked:

> And I have reasons, Madam, for disliking *him*. And why am
> I—
> This quickness upon me, interrupted my Mother, is not to
> be borne! I am gone, and your Father comes, if *I* can do no
> good with you.
> O Madam, I would rather die, than—
> She put her hand to my mouth. —No peremptoriness,
> Clary Harlowe. [I, 114]

Later Arabella performs the same gesture more brutally, stuff-
ing her handkerchief ("very rudely") into Clarissa's mouth
while Clarissa is talking (II, 46).

Other forms of interruption reinforce these acts of conversa-
tional violence. After "perverse" Clarissa is locked in her
room, for example, the messages she sends down to her family
are either sent back unread or "torn in pieces." Her outside
correspondence—with Anna, and of course with Lovelace—is
prohibited. (The real reader is implicated along with the
heroine by this prohibition: we feel it—as a threat to narrative.
If the letters to Anna cease, for instance, so does the fiction
itself: our source of information about Clarissa's "Story" is

likewise "cut off." It is with relief then that we see her skirt the Harlowes' ruling.) The linguistic constraint Clarissa suffers is thus a first index to her loss of power at Harlowe-Place. Because she will not signify compliance with parental authority ("Will you not, can you not, speak as I would have you speak?" cries her demoralized, simpering mother), the Harlowes try to cut her out of the realm of signifying altogether. Not surprisingly, she in turn becomes increasingly desperate *to* articulate, and increasingly vulnerable to those who, through the medium of the letter, allow her this possibility. The letters to Anna continue, surreptitiously, and a new secret correspondence, with Lovelace, begins.

There is yet another dimension to the Harlowes' "strange politics," however. A more insidious kind of linguistic interruption—semantic—is instituted against Clarissa. The world of Harlowe-Place is one, above all, where meaning is skewed. The hermeneutic trap the family designs for the heroine is twofold: she can neither prevent them from reading arbitrary, incriminating meanings into her own words and behavior, nor can she make sense out of theirs—their speeches and gestures seem equally "unnatural" and unprecedented. This situation marks a deepening of Clarissa's predicament— one that in some ways goes beyond the simple, even primitive prohibition the Harlowes have tried to put on her speaking. The interpretative process itself is revealed on two counts as nightmarishly defective.

Clarissa finds, first of all, that everything she says and does is immediately susceptible to "misconstruction" or "misrepresentation" by her relatives. The utterances she does manage to make—both within the primary code of language itself and within a second language of gesture (in Clarissa's terms, the two codes of "Word" and "Deed")—are robbed of the significance that she intends. What Clarissa here encounters for the first time, though she does not yet fully understand the implications, is the malleability inherent in her own use of signs.

Her understanding is limited because she believes, innocently enough, in a correspondence between utterance and truth, between the outward sign and the inward reality. Clarissa's basic linguistic assumption is that words embody, absolutely and transparently, the inner life of the speaker. As she reveals to Anna, she holds implicitly to a myth of language, which she applies first to her own discourse, and then by extension to the speech of others. Utterance, she assumes, is grounded in being and truth. Words come from within and express the soul. They have a "natural" or privileged relation to the actual; they have an exact correspondence to the inner person. Typically Clarissa uses a body metaphor to register this belief: language flows from the "heart." The "dictating heart" is the image she uses to account for signification itself. Her own speech, she imagines, is both motivated and constrained by the "authority" of the heart. And hence the message clothed in language must needs be as clear, as translucent, as the heart itself. When her family distort her words, they distort the core of her being: "O, that they did but know my heart!—It shall sooner burst, than voluntarily, uncompelled, undriven, dictate a measure that shall cast a slur either upon Them, or upon my Sex" (I, 209). Richardson's—and Lovelace's—fanciful etymological linking of "cor-respondence" with the communication of "hearts" is to the point here: Clarissa's figure of the dictating heart reveals her desire to "naturalize" discourse—to invest it with a kind of absolute truthfulness, the truth of human presence.

The Harlowes, of course, take advantage of Clarissa's simple semantics—heartlessly. They repeatedly ignore her intended meaning, the "heart" of the matter, and instead produce their own creative glosses on her words. Ill will alone conditions these interpretative acts. "One may see, my dear," Clarissa writes to her friend, "the force of hatred, which misrepresents all things" (I, 271). She finds that her relations "make a handle of my words against me, when I am not permitted to speak in my own defence" (I, 175). The situation is baffling and disorienting: the heroine must stand by, powerlessly, while her apparently clear statements are transformed, through perverse twists of interpretation, into self-incriminations. Simple articulations become suddenly multivalent. Thus Clarissa's refusal of Mr. Solmes's proposal, for example, spawns multiple meanings: it becomes at once the sign of her general "disobedience" to the parental will, her "pervicacity," her "pride," and most damningly and illogically, her "prepossession" for Lovelace. The heroine's intended message, delimiting solely her reaction to Solmes, is covered over, reinscribed, with secondary (unintended) meanings. This chain of signification is constructed arbitrarily: it reflects no essential truth, only the Harlowes' preferred reading of Clarissa's case. (She has already sworn, of course, that her rejection of Solmes does not imply desire for Lovelace, and that indeed she will never marry at all if allowed to forego Solmes's proposal.)

As for written communication, Clarissa's letters are treated equally problematically. After she is locked up, those despairing notes she sends down to her family are likewise subjected to "invidious applications." They become what semioticians call second-order signifying systems.[4] That is, they yield up their original content to interpretations imposed after the fact. What the letter actually says is overlooked; the "gloss," which may seem wildly irrelevant, is all. Thus, Clarissa's message repeating her wish for the "Single Life" (I, 170) is made over by its readers into proof of her guilty affection for Lovelace. When her "justly incensed" father replies to it, he occults the original sense entirely, and reads it allegorically—as a "natural" mark of his daughter's "disobedience." The letter thus comes to signify something other than its own message.

4. Roland Barthes, *Mythologies*, trans. Annette Lavers (London: Jonathan Cape, 1972), p. 114.

Its existence in the world, not what it tries to say, is what is significant: the very presence of the letter signals Clarissa's supposed iniquity. "Your letter," writes Mr. Harlowe, "but upbraids me for my past indulgence" (I, 176). Another letter, to Arabella, is treated similarly, Clarissa's appeal for understanding being interpreted as trickery. "You are a fond foolish girl with all your wisdom," Arabella concludes; "Your letter shews *that* enough in twenty places" (I, 205). Arabella's banal choice of verb, "shews"—a word that enforces a metonymic connection without specifying the logical grounds for such a relationship—exposes the full arbitrariness of her interpretation.

Confronting such consistent semantic distortion but not comprehending the hermeneutic politics involved, Clarissa typically compounds the situation by trying to say *more*. She falls into a kind of desperate metastatement when she explains how she wishes to be understood: "Pray do not put the worst, but the best constructions upon my proposals, when you have them reported to you. Indeed I mean the best. I have no subterfuges, no arts, no intentions, but to keep to the Letter of them" (I, 322). But every new articulation is open to the same unconstrained exegesis. And such instructions to the reader carry no weight in the world of Harlowe-Place.

To this deformation of Clarissa's speech and writing one must add the deformation of a certain "discourse of the body" through which she also tries to articulate. Again, the epistolary novel always encourages such a movement between different signifying codes: what happens within the system of linguistic exchange is a paradigm for what happens in other systems of symbolic exchange. At one point, Clarissa implores Mrs. Harlowe to ignore James and Arabella and "let *my* actions, not *their* misrepresentations (as I am sure by the disgraceful prohibitions I have met with has been the case) speak for me" (I, 110). She believes in the expressivity of "countenance"; she thinks that, just like words, faces and other physical features are indices of the "heart" within. Thus for her, Solmes's gargoyle-like visage is a "natural" marker for his inner moral corruption, and she despises him accordingly. As well as words, she uses a language of expression and gesture when she communicates with her relatives, yet this code of signification is also continuously vulnerable to unexpected readings. At the same time that Clarissa's speech is interrupted in the conversation with Mrs. Harlowe, the heroine's physical gestures are read opposite to the way she intends. The conventional code of the body is subverted, as Mrs. Harlowe interprets Clarissa's acts of deference as ill temper.

> I don't love to see the girl look so sullen.
> Indeed, Madam, I am not sullen. —And I arose, and, turning from her, drew out my handkerchief; for the tears ran down my cheeks. . . .
> One of the most provoking things in the world is, to have people cry for what they can help!   [I, 130]

When Clarissa curtseys "with reverence" her mother cries out, "Mock me not with outward gestures of respect. The heart, Clary, is what I want." Clarissa here can do nothing but try again with words, and swears, "Indeed, Madam, you have it." "Fine talking!" ripostes Mrs. Harlowe. In this surreal dialogue, which continues for several pages, the heroine is forced back and forth between the code of the body and the code of language—but both are equally insufficient to the occasion. And when she throws herself at her mother's feet, intending to symbolize her love and supplication with this "natural" gesture, her intention is again transformed: "Limbs so supple; Will so stubborn!" (I, 131). Here and everywhere, Clarissa cannot make her body *say* what she wants it to say.[5]

5. In "The Countenance You Show Me: Reading the Passions in the Eighteenth Century," *Georgia Review*, 32 (1978), 758–73, Alan T. McKenzie suggests that a highly specific "grammar" of conventional facial expressions

All of this distortion is of course a distressing premonition of her "usage" at the hands of Lovelace. In the most profound sense, Clarissa tends to become a kind of text for her family—a rhetorical event. Her very body is inscribed by them with symbolic content, and it is not a content she can in any way control. Against her will she is made over into a sign. In her own poignant phrase, she is "circumscribed" by them, written around. Their interpretations condition her alienation and confusion. Yet the significance the Harlowes claim to find *in* their daughter, what they read in her, is always a reflection only of their own desires and fears. The heroine's inner experience has nothing to do, particularly, with the messages others find embodied in her. The real self remains a cipher ("Cl. H.," she calls herself), unknown. For the Harlowes' appendage, Solmes, the cipher fills up with economic meaning: he links Clarissa, metonymically, with the Harlowe fortune, and this is her sole significance for him. For the Harlowes themselves, she is a more complex sign, a figure they inscribe with enigmatic insecurities, sexual phantasms, and aggressive desires. The model of reading at work here is active, Barthesian. The family, in effect, *produce* Clarissa, through a collective act of hermeneutic violence. They invest her words, her behavior, with incriminating significance, and then, mind-bogglingly, use this projected significance to *prove* her innate corruption. The Harlowes justify their readings with an appeal to Nature: Clarissa, they claim, is "naturally perverse," as her behavior "shews." The interpretative act, however, is always a denaturing act, for the real self is abolished in the process. As Clarissa's incarceration suggests, the Harlowes'

---

existed in the eighteenth century. See in particular his discussion of Charles Le Brun's scheme for depicting the passions (1698) and its influence on eighteenth-century English artists and authors, pp. 762–66. The Harlowes, of course, disrupt any notion of systematic communication through gesture or expression.

authority is not grounded in Nature, but in intimidation. They shackle her physically; they shackle her metaphorically, by treating her as a text, and reading her according to their own desire. Lovelace, of course, will do the same.

Once again an instability in human sign systems makes possible the abusive situation in Harlowe-Place. The absence of "Nature" from those codes through which Clarissa tries to communicate conditions her predicament. The kneeling scene with her mother just noted is an archetypal demonstration of this absence. While Clarissa assumes that genuflection means humility, love, and so on—gesture and significance being indissolubly wedded—Mrs. Harlowe's new reading exposes the conventional, or social nature of the symbolism involved, and likewise, that social meanings can be suspended at any time. The scene carries the *éclat* that one associates with the anthropological case study. Yet if the readings imposed on Clarissa in the early part of the fiction bespeak a fallible hermeneutic system, her own attempt to interpret the world results in a parallel confrontation with indeterminacy. A kind of mirror-effect is working here: at Harlowe-Place the lack of hermeneutic constraint makes it possible for Clarissa's actions to be taken in the worst light; yet the same lack also plunges her into her private trauma of reading. While others read her oppressively, they also undermine her ability to read *them*. The Harlowes scramble their own signals. Like those she tries to send out, the messages Clarissa receives—both linguistic and behavioral—are thus invariably problematic.

The challenge to Clarissa's own interpretative skill comes first in the realm of speech. Before, as we have seen, her family has interrupted her effort to say what is happening; they seem also, however, to be muddling and disrupting their own conversation just to confuse her further. She frequently cannot make out what they are saying to her. On the physical plane, the utterances of others are often curiously incomplete or incomprehensible. There are several times after she is locked in her room, for instance, when Clarissa can hear the voices of her relations, but, as in a dream, cannot catch what is being said. She believes at one point that her Aunt Hervey speaks in her favor: "But I heard not the words" (I, 349). When her mother raves at her, syntax is ruptured—"*Strange perverseness!* were the only words I heard of a sentence that she angrily pronounced" (I, 148). Her conversations were Bella, however, represent this phenomenon in its most extreme form. Typically, her sister breaks off in mid-sentence, thus leaving Clarissa in a state of suspense about her meaning. The heroine does not know how to close off the utterance: "O, thou art a—And down she flung without saying what" (I, 347). In a similar vein, Arabella frustrates her sister's will to understanding by making maddeningly random, nonsignificant "noises." "Bella [was] all the while humming a tune, and opening this book and that, without meaning; but saying nothing" (I, 335). Again, while Clarissa is trying to compose a letter to the family, Arabella breaks her concentration by doodling on a harpsichord and once more "humming" (I, 323). Bella's sounds are a parody of meaningful speech (Lovelace will later be described by Mrs. Harlowe as "buzzing" around Clarissa), yet in a deeper sense, they are also a revelation of the nature of discourse in Clarissa's world. She cannot recuperate the language of the family; they reduce her, in effect, to the preverbal condition of the infant—hearing but not comprehending. And Clarissa seems to share, as a result, some of the primal anxiety of that state: "I wept."

Behavior, like language, is similarly incoherent. The actions of Clarissa's family are consistently at odds with her expectations. They are illegible. It is impossible to read conventional significance into anything that goes on among the Harlowes. Clarissa, for example, has a number of models of intelligibility—in particular familial and sexual codes of meaning—which she uses to order her world. She assumes a certain syntax of behavior. Members of families, she believes, normally relate to each other in a certain way—the sexes likewise. As in everything, she naturalizes this syntax. And once again, she does not perceive the conventional nature of the codes she uses. In her letters to Anna Howe, thus, she makes much of the fact that her family's actions toward her betray "natural" bonds of kinship. Mothers and fathers, she believes, are called upon by "Nature" to be "tender" to their offspring; brothers and sisters are meant to show "brotherly" and "sisterly" love to their siblings. But the Harlowes' unaccountable cruelty subverts Clarissa's biological notions—her faith in the deep, magical ties of blood relationship. Her father's behavior, she tells Anna, is "unnatural," not that which one would expect from a *father*. Likewise, her mother fails to show "truly maternal tenderness." Clarissa repeatedly pleads with James and Arabella for "brotherly" and "sisterly" affection, but to no avail. Characteristically, she falls into tautology, trying to reconcile biological relationship with her need for emotional support: "Should not Sisters *be* Sisters to each other?" (I, 91). The redundancy is grounded in failure of insight. What Clarissa does not grasp yet, of course, is that her assumption about "being a sister" is purely conventional—part of a sentimental ideology of kinship. The Harlowes expose familial obligation itself as a fictional construct—to Clarissa's distress.

Linked to this denaturing of kinship function, though present in a less insistent manner, is the Harlowes' suspension of conventional sexual roles. Clarissa again assumes a "natural" distinction between male and female behavior, and again her expectations are thrown into chaos by what really goes on at Harlowe-Place. James and Arabella are the primary figures here. From Clarissa's perspective, both seem to cross supposedly fixed sexual boundaries in a distressing way. James's manner appears to her strangely "effeminate." By contrast, Arabella's treatment of her—though essentially the same as James's—seems "masculine." Clarissa assumes that certain psychological characteristics, such as the ability to "compassionate," are the exclusive property of one or the other of the sexes. Arabella's cruelty, her imitation of "the rougher manners of men," makes her seem to Clarissa a kind of sexual freak. Overhearing an argument about her in which all the female Harlowes except Arabella are shouted down, Clarissa meditates on the nature of the sexes and develops a contorted and ultimately nonsensical interpretation of her sister's soul:

> *Female* accents I could distinguish the drowned ones to be. O my dear! What a hard-hearted Sex is the other! Children of the same parents, how came they by their cruelty? —Do they get it by travel? Do they get it by conversation with one another? —Or how do they get it? —Yet my Sister, too, is as hard-hearted as any of them. But this may be no exception neither: For she has been thought to be masculine in her air, and in her spirit. She has then perhaps, a soul of the *other* Sex in a body of *ours*. [II, 216]

Clarissa (unlike Anna, who has a much livelier grasp of the arbitrariness of sexual differences) is unable to conceive of the social, conditional nature of sexual roles. For her, maleness and femaleness imply different psychological predispositions—absolutely and eternally. Clarissa's naiveté is again damaging: her assumptions about "natural" male and female behavior make her perpetually vulnerable to those who suspend conventional roles. (Most disastrously Lovelace—with his penchant for transvestite stratagems—and the "masculine" Sinclair will later exploit her in just this way.)

In the realms of familial and sexual behavior, thus, as in the linguistic realm, Clarissa's accustomed models of intelligibility do not hold. It must be stressed again, however, that here, and even long after the flight away from Harlowe-Place, Clarissa herself does not understand what has gone wrong in her world. She knows something terrible and strange is happening to her perceptions, but cannot explain what. The Harlowes have systematically challenged her ability to construct meaning—out of both "Words" and "Deeds." As a result she experiences profound defamiliarization—an existential equivalent to what Viktor Shklovsky has called the *ostranenie* effect in narrative, a "making strange." She becomes anxious and frightened. The actions of her "Friends" do not fit her sense of the natural syntax of human life; they seem ungrammatical. Like a native speaker hearing a nonsense sentence, Clarissa experiences what linguists would describe as a "bizarreness reaction." The Harlowes' uncanny meanness leaves her "speechless." But she is dumb on another count. She has no comprehension of the hermeneutic dynamic in which she is caught. She does not question at this point her own skill as a reader, or her faith in the essential legibility of Nature. She trusts the text—for all its aberrations—and her own powers of exegesis.

Apart thus from a few moments of self-abnegation—when indeed she wonders if her relatives are right about her "pride" and "pervicacity"—she becomes more and more implicated in the world of signs and interpretation. The secret communication with Anna and Lovelace, as I noted before, reflects her desire for speech: as the Harlowes interrupt her "Story," she tries to articulate it elsewhere. Yet there is a sense in which this movement only compounds the hermeneutic problem, and deepens the heroine's vulnerability. Before turning to Lovelace and the fulfillment of Clarissa's catastrophe of reading, we must say a few words finally about Anna Howe, and the crucial correspondence with her. "My own dear Miss Howe," it turns out, unknowingly contributes as much as anyone else to Clarissa's mistakes of reading, and to the greater peril into which she falls.

The irony here is particularly acute, of course, because the correspondence with Anna would seem to provide Clarissa with an avenue of escape, an outlet for free speech. For the real reader, the epistolary dialogue between Clarissa and Anna

is the only break from the claustrophobic situation at
Harlowe-Place. Amid the dislocations and shocks of the fictional world, it seems a gesture toward the truth—toward a
more normal and recognizable human experience—and we
read it, at least at first, with a sense of relief. Clarissa thinks of
the correspondence as part of that great discourse of the
"heart" which is everywhere her goal. Her letters embody, she
trusts, the truth of her feelings. Anna appears receptive to
Clarissa's attempt at self-expression: "Write to me therefore,
my dear, the whole of your Story" (I, 3). Anna expresses her
willingness to *listen,* for she loves "as never woman loved
another" (I, 4). The innocent mythology of friendship with
which Anna and Clarissa surround their correspondence is
deceptive, however. In the world of *Clarissa,* even this dialogue of "hearts" is touched by aggression. Anna reads Clarissa's letters, of course; but she also reads Clarissa herself—just
as much, in fact, as any of the Harlowes do. The more of their
letters we see the clearer it becomes that Anna herself is imposing certain "constructions" on Clarissa's words and actions.
Clarissa indeed invites this: she defers to her friend's interpretations. Clarissa yields to Anna's sharper "penetration": "I am
almost *afraid* to beg of you, and yet I repeatedly *do,* to give
way to that charming spirit, whenever it rises to your pen,
which smiles, yet goes to the quick of my fault. What patient
shall be afraid of a probe in so delicate a hand?" (II, 155).
(The imagistic conflation of interpretation with physical
aggression—probing, prodding, entering—will become even
more insistent later, in relation to Lovelace.[6]) But Clarissa's
passivity is dangerous. In the all-important matter of her feeling about Lovelace, for example, Anna's reading of the situation is utterly compromising. Already in the tenth letter of the
novel Miss Howe—an aggressive exegete—thinks she detects

6. See Leo Braudy, "Penetration and Impenetrability in *Clarissa,*" in *New
Approaches to Eighteenth-Century Literature* (Selected Papers from the English
Institute), ed. Phillip Harth (New York: Columbia University Press, 1974).

"Hints" in Clarissa's letters of an attraction to Lovelace. Clarissa makes no expression of such emotion; Anna leaps to conclusions. Speaking of her friend's feeling, she is sure "it will come out to be LOVE" (I, 67). Lovelace, she writes, is a "charming fellow," worthy of favor. With mock seriousness, Anna says she fears that her very words will cause Clarissa, reading them, to "glow." She makes an appeal finally (and ironically) to that touchstone of truth—her friend's "heart." "Yet, my dear, don't you find at your heart somewhat unusual make it go throb, throb, throb, as you read just here?" (I, 67). Whether consciously or no, Anna's interpretation—which appropriates even Clarissa's physiological response—is an imposition. Miss Howe here writes Clarissa into an erotic scenario of her own devising. (Psychologically speaking, there is much to suggest that Anna displaces onto the heroine her own erotic attraction to Lovelace.) The rhetoric of Clarissa's "better pilot," like that of the "controuling" Harlowes, seems designed precisely to direct, to determine, to circumscribe.

Clarissa is pitifully susceptible to Anna's rhetoric. Without Clarissa realizing it, Anna's letters in effect subvert her mythology of the dictating heart. Language itself dictates to the heart, rather than the other way around. Her friend's irresponsible suggestions have a curiously mediating influence on Clarissa's own feelings. Though in subsequent letters she denies "the imputed *glow* or *throb*" (I, 261), Anna's words have their effect; they condition a subtle, but growing emotional entanglement with Lovelace. The "construction" does not reflect reality, but creates it; the linguistic act becomes prophetic, rather than mimetic. Clarissa begins to act out her friend's fantasy—by writing letters to Lovelace secretly, by admitting him clandestinely to her presence, by behaving, in short, in exactly the conventional manner of the enamoured and flirtatious young woman. Reading Anna's letters, Clarissa, paradoxically, is in fact reading Anna's reading—of the state of her own feeling. Her tendency is to consume the interpretation, to let it penetrate her. Before, Clarissa has not experienced a "prepossession" for Lovelace, but as soon as the potential for desire is articulated by another, desire becomes a possibility—in her own heart.

For the real reader, this effect of phenomenological reversal—where the letter one receives seems to condition, rather than simply reflect, one's situation—is intensified by the peculiar nature of the epistolary novel itself. As we move through the great pattern of letters, utterance (because it is the only real event taking place) seems to have an anticipatory, even affective force. With a kind of tragic fatality characters' speculations about the future invariably come true. *Clarissa* impresses on us, thus, an odd sensation of linguistic causality. What is written of—even in jest or in a moment of thoughtlessness—comes into being. Clarissa's family, for instance, speak obsessively about her imminent "ruin" if she associates with Lovelace; and she *is* in fact ruined, but not in the way anyone expects. Anna, distressingly enough, is attuned to the peculiar relationship between the linguistic formulation and future events. Just after describing Clarissa's "throbbing" heart—and in effect writing it into being—she calls attention, through a powerful historical and literary allusion, to the potentially prophetic element in her own articulation: "But," she concludes her warning to her friend, "as the Roman augur said, Caesar, beware of the Ides of March!" (1, 67). For the reader outside the fiction, the allusion functions not so much as a real warning, but ironically, as an intimation that disaster is inescapable. We are left with the sense that Anna's implicit doomsaying is in fact conditioning Clarissa's doom. Once we review her words in light of the final catastrophe, the effect is eerie. Almost *because* Clarissa has been linked to Caesar, her death seems unavoidable; it takes on, retroactively, a kind of historical necessity. But *Clarissa* is filled with such unnerving instances of apparent word-magic. To cite, finally, one of the more macabre: Clarissa's exclamation in Volume II, when she faces an unwanted interview with Solmes—"O that a deep sleep of twenty-four hours would seize my faculties!" (II, 193)—comes true quite dreadfully later on when she is drugged and sexually abused by Lovelace and Sinclair. Like a character in folklore, the heroine makes an "accidental wish" and it is granted, in a horrible fashion—by the narrative itself. Such moments may be, of course, Richardson's more or less vulgar attempts to build dramatic irony into his text, but they reinforce, again, our sense of the mediating power of the verbal construct.

Even at the very moment when Clarissa believes herself free from odious "construction"—in her correspondence with Anna Howe—she is in fact falling deeper into a linguistic trap. Anna too subjects her to interpretation; and as the Harlowes' oppressions increase, Clarissa becomes more than willing to let her friend "write the script" for her. So great is Clarissa's investment in the linguistic circuit, the world of the letter, that she remains blind to its peril. In accordance with Anna's scenario, she opens herself soon enough to the exegesis of yet another, even more dangerous "Intelligencer." "O my friend," writes Anna, "depend upon it, you are in danger. Depend upon it, whether you know it or not, you are a little in for't" (I, 66).

5

Denatured Signs

In the beginning Clarissa is drawn to Lovelace because he lets her speak. He offers her a correspondence, and out of her great and desperate desire—for discourse itself—she falls into it with him. For his part, the strategy is one of slow entrapment. He plays precisely, masterfully, on her desire for language, on her tremendous will toward signification. He acts the part of that "Lithuanian lover" whom he speaks of to Belford in a bizarrely pedantic etymological footnote, as an "*auditore*"—a "listener" (VII, 16). He is eager to hear the "truth."

When Clarissa agrees to meet secretly with Lovelace in the garden, he chooses the most seductive and ingenious of tactics: he allows her to interrupt *him*. In their first encounter, when he jumps out from behind the woodhouse, he tries to pledge his love, and Clarissa replies with "And pray, Sir, let me interrupt you in my turn." (I, 259). He does. In the final garden meeting, which leads to abduction, the two talk wildly to each other—but Lovelace still allows her significant moments of expansion: she breaks in upon him ("interrupted I") at several important places in the conversation. At such moments, Lovelace becomes passive, attentive, sycophantic.

Clarissa is taken by surprise—and powerfully attracted—by such apparent speechlessness. In the time between the first and last meeting, Lovelace makes himself even more attractive by contracting—or telling Clarissa he has contracted—the perfect symbolic illness: he becomes "hoarse" after sitting all night by the Harlowes' garden wall, and "has no voice" for several days thereafter. Later, whenever Lovelace wishes to reassure her of his honorable intentions, he will grant her a similar power of speech, and give her a temporary illusion of "authority." "He was very attentive to all I said;" wide-eyed Clarissa writes, "never offering to interrupt me once" (III, 8).

Most important, however, is that in these early stages Lovelace seems to take what Clarissa says at face value. When they talk he does not put glosses on her words; he appears to accept her determinations, her intended meaning, as binding upon him. He adds oaths of his own to what she says— swearing he will act by her expressed wishes, and that if she does in fact "go off" with him, he will not impose on her, but will take her to a place of refuge, Miss Howe's or elsewhere. Lovelace seems to Clarissa, unlike any of the Harlowes, to read her "heart." She worries occasionally that he is too glib, that indeed he may lack a "heart" himself (and be controlled instead by the deracinating dictates of the "head"), but she trusts him at this point more than not. He seems to give her what she has lacked—a chance at speech, uncorrupted by "misrepresentation." As Richardson the "Editor" puts it in the summary of Volume I, "He greatly engages her confidence (*as he had designed*) by his respectful behaviour" (I, 356).

The long curve of the fiction between the abduction and Clarissa's rape is also a fall, of course—her fall into Lovelace's hermeneutic snare. The fall begins in a failure of interpretation, in confused voices that Clarissa cannot hear well enough to understand—the feigned alarms of Joseph Leman. It ends in a similar failure, in a vision of "flitting" female shapes, too "imperfectly" seen to identify—the prostitutes at Sinclair's.

Denatured Signs

Above all, Clarissa's fall is designed for her; it is an orchestrated movement into increasingly incoherent realms. Through "Art," Lovelace destroys Clarissa's sense of "Nature" itself, her ground of meaning. He systematically violates her faith in the essential legibility of experience; he violates her faith in the natural significance of things. This disordering—the disruption of all of Clarissa's models of reading—coincides, ultimately, with a more basic kind of interference. The violence in the world of signs, motivated by Lovelace, modulates into sexual violence. The interruption of meaning that Clarissa is made to experience at Sinclair's culminates in an actual interruption of her person, in the moment of rape. Lovelace breaks that intimate, ideal bond she sees between "Nature" and the sign; he breaks, at last, her body itself.

In terms of the extended drama of interpretation which we have been following, Lovelace's treatment of Clarissa seems similar in many respects to what she has already suffered at Harlowe-Place. The difference is one of intensity. She moves one might say, from the realm of the anxiety dream to the realm of nightmare. For the reader outside the fiction, the move also takes on the qualities of the nightmare. Our sense of Clarissa's extremity increases exponentially because now, more than ever before, we become party to Lovelace's own correspondence with Belford, and thus receive directly his reading of the heroine. As John Preston has noted, the real reader's own feeling of powerlessness—in face of the implacability of Lovelace's plots and our inability to affect the narrative situation—grows in proportion to the heroine's steady loss of choice and freedom. "[*Clarissa*] asks us to recognize the act of reading as a reflection of the existential crisis generated within the novel itself."[1]

Most important, perhaps, Lovelace's letters to Belford make

---

1. John Preston, *The Created Self: The Role of the Reader in Eighteenth-Century Fiction* (London: Heinemann, 1970), p. 61.

visible again the linguistic dimensions of Clarissa's suffering. As she remarks about their natures generally, Clarissa's and Lovelace's ways of using language are "different in *essentials.*" If her correspondence with Anna makes explicit her faith in the discourse of the "heart," and in a natural relation existing between the sign and the thing signified, between gesture and an inner state of being, Lovelace's writings to Belford reveal his distance from Clarissa's persistent logocentrism. Like Clarissa, ironically enough, Lovelace is a prodigy of language—a linguist, a ready "scribbler," "excessively voluble." But his involvement in the realm of signification has never been subject to inner or outer "controul"—to epistemological constraints. No meaning, for him, is naturally grounded. Any sign can be dislocated from its ostensible referent; every type of communicating code can be exploited. Lovelace is preeminently aware of the autonymous power of the utterance, and revels in it. He loves to produce fantastical messages which others, innocently, read as the truth. Lovelace knows that the text one writes has no obligation to any objective realm of things; in fact, he has internalized absolutely the priority of "Art" over "Nature." The construct, the artifice, subsumes the natural. "Nature" ceases to exist; the plot is all.

The world Lovelace inhabits is ultimately a world of language alone, a world of reading. Commentators on *Clarissa* have seized often on his need to dramatize experience in terms of the literary texts he has read. In the letters to Belford, he repeatedly casts himself and others as characters in a great, ongoing imaginary drama—one that reflects back upon a vast repertoire of texts: Shakespeare, Dryden, the Restoration playwrights. Above all, his perceptions of Clarissa are mediated by literary examples. With a kind of high-handed ease, he justifies his behavior with citations lifted from books and plays. Mark Kinkead-Weeks writes thus that "in the idea-world of Restoration drama, Lovelace finds an echo of his needs and a convenient notation of his feelings. He echoes its view of the sex war; and both the cynicism of its Comedy, and the indulgence in the stormier passions of its Tragedy."[2] So great is Lovelace's obsession with textual mediacy, that he is led at times into absurd ontological reversals, as when he describes his and Clarissa's involvement in terms of literary "works" that do not exist at all, except in his imagination—"The Quarrelsome Lovers," "The History of the Lady and the Penknife."

The fascination with literary artifacts, however, is but an extension of his relation to language generally. The way Lovelace lets literary convention determine the melodramatic poses he strikes for Clarissa points to a greater syndrome: a willingness to let linguistic formulas in general shape his attitude toward others. Mottos, extracts, instantaneous epigrams—all mediate between him and other people. Pieces of articulation take on a conditioning, almost talismanic force for Lovelace. Certain utterances—some drawn from historical sources, some made up on the spot—thus reappear like burden in the letters to Belford; they are pulled in to lend hokey "authority" to his interpretation of events. The odious Popean tag, "Every woman is at heart a rake," is an example of such an utterance: the dictum constrains Lovelace's own woman-hating gloss on Clarissa's "heart"—

> One argument let me plead in proof of my assertion; That even we Rakes love modesty in a woman; while the modest women as they are accounted (that is to say, the *slyest*) love, and generally prefer, an impudent man. Whence can this be, but from a likeness in nature? And this made the poet say, That every woman is a Rake in her heart. It concerns them, by their *actions*, to prove the contrary, if they can. [III, 115]

Likewise, all the supposed "maxims" of the "Rake's Creed"—of which Lovelace speaks as if it had a tangible, institu-

2. Mark Kinkead-Weekes, *Samuel Richardson: Dramatic Novelist* (Ithaca: Cornell University Press, 1973), p. 147.

tionalized reality—are deployed similarly: as "articles" that condition the behavior of man to woman. Lovelace's obsessive analysis of events in terms of real and invented "maxims" bespeaks again a pervasive linguistic determinism, an anti-mimesis. His linguistic practice inverts the "natural" referential sequence assumed by Clarissa—the flow of meaning from world to word. Discourse takes priority; it formulates the human situation. For Lovelace, language (and soon enough, all secondary codes of significance too) is thus not a re-presentation of experience, but experience itself. Nothing, apart from other pieces of language—the great interlocking system of texts that he has read—has the power to control one's use of the code of meaning. The very heart, in Clarissa's term, is "perjur'd."

Though alienated from "Nature," Lovelace's constructions are compelling nonetheless. He infuses them with the aggressive force of his personality. "What signifies power, if we do not exert it?" (IV, 135). As becomes more and more clear as *Clarissa* progresses, he backs up words with an implicit physical threat. His fantasy, late in the fiction, of abusing and ultimately seeing Belford consumed (Belford has thwarted him on some matter relating to Clarissa) is arabesque and ridiculous, but it also reveals a scarifying potential for violence lying behind his words: "Confound thee for a malicious devil! I wish thou wert a post-horse, and I upon the back of thee! How would I whip and spur, and harrow up thy clumsy sides, till I made thee a ready-roasted, ready-flayed, mess of dog's meat; all the hounds in the county howling after thee, to wait my dismounting, in order to devour thee peace-meal; life still throbbing in each churned mouthful!" (VI, 306). The desire to control others through language is Lovelace's ruling passion. The artifices of this "Male-Delinquent" succeed to the extent that they are grounded in a willingness, however facetiously articulated, to terrorize.

Like the Harlowes, Lovelace reads Clarissa, and like theirs, his reading has nothing to do with what she is. What she is, of course, is the "Story" that never gets told—of which the text of *Clarissa* itself, as we will see, is the fractured symbol. Lovelace limns Clarissa; he produces her; he fills her image with meaning. His actual interception and reading of her letters to Anna, midway in the fiction, is, as always, a paradigm for that act of interpretation he engages in in regard to her person. She is the great text to which he applies all his skill in the "science of reading men"; she is his favorite rhetorical *topos*, an inexhaustible locus for exegesis.

Unlike that of Solmes, the thesis Lovelace locates in Clarissa is not economic, but endlessly sexual: "My predominant passion is *Girl*, not *Gold*" (III, 63). Clarissa is identified with this italicized essence; her body is a transcription of the text of "Woman" itself. Lovelace's correspondence with Belford is in large part a continuing monograph on the nature of "Woman," a gloss on this most exciting of constructs. The linguistic token sets off a chain of signification for Lovelace: "Woman" is everywhere the sign of untrammeled sexuality, vulnerability, inner corruption, thrilling and debased weakness. Again, Lovelace marshals all the pieces of stereotypically misogynistic discourse he knows in support of the symbolic chain. The classic patriarchal texts of Western culture, including Scripture itself, provide him, not surprisingly, with much fodder. "Thus I have read in some of the philosophers [Ecclesiasticus, the "Editor" informs us], *That no wickedness is comparable to the wickedness of a woman*" (III, 115). "If she be a *woman*, and *love* me, I shall surely catch her once tripping: For Love was ever a traitor to its harbourer: And Love *within*, and I *without*, she will be *more* than woman, as the poet says, or I *less* than man, if I succeed not" (III, 95). Again: "Rinaldo indeed in Ariosto put the Mantuan Knight's Cup of trial from him, which was to be the proof of his Wife's chastity— This was his argument for forbearing the experiment: "Why should I seek a thing I should be loth to find? My Wife is a Woman. The Sex is frail"

(III, 92). And at the last, the patriarchal text sanctions male supremacy: "I have read in some place, *that the woman was made for the man*, not *the man for the woman*" (III, 90). The meaning-effect that Lovelace creates, and validates with elaborate intertextual play, is of course fantastical and arbitrary—there is no such thing as this "Woman," no referent for it in the world of persons, indeed, the world of women. The construct has nothing to do with any real woman, such as Clarissa; it is an empty sign—a banal linguistic site around which all the "maxims" of the Rake occlude.

Yet Clarissa is made to stand for the entire chain of significance that "Woman" entails. Lovelace inscribes her, in letter after letter, with the phantasmic concept; he makes her over as the sign of "Femality" itself. She is forced to carry the metaphoric burden of everything that he and his "Rakes' Confraternity" have ever said about mythic "Woman." She is weighted with a significance over which she has no control.

Lovelace's fiction of her nature absorbs every detail of her behavior. Her protestations after the abduction, and ultimate refusal of him, are interpreted by Lovelace in light of the construct—as sly come-ons, as marks of hypocrisy and secret pride. Even her embarrassed blushing (part of the conventional discourse of the body itself) is made over by her persecutor into a signal of hidden desire. Lovelace's surprisingly modern analysis of the blush as deceptive sign ("The women are told how much their blushes heighten their graces: They practise for them therefore: Blushes come as readily when they call for them, as their Tears" [v, 2])—with its intimations also of the Freudian notion of the displacement upward—should not distract us from the fact that he is imposing meaning, arbitrarily, upon her. Lovelace's model of interpretation is founded upon binary opposition: he assumes that Clarissa's words and gestures automatically mean the opposite of what she seems to intend. Thus the conventional sign relation (blush = modesty) is transformed into a new relation that accords with the fiction of "Woman's" intrusive sexuality (blush = eros). Too many critics, indeed, have tended to read Clarissa's behavior in the light of Lovelace's classically misogynistic model, that is, assuming that a subliminal sexual content is part of her "message." Yet whether or not it is remains indeterminate. The fiction does not clarify the nature of Clarissa's desire. To read her blush, then, as Lovelace does, is to produce a meaning for it, but one that has no *necessary* relation to truth, which remains elusive, absent.

Metaphoric aggression is, then, Lovelace's first and most basic affront against Clarissa. It becomes the prototype for every other kind of abuse he wages against her—all of which involve a similar hermeneutic dislocation of the sign away from "Nature." His gloss on "Clarissa Harlowe"—its range of meaning overlaps in every particular with that of "Woman"—represents a creative elision between terms: it is masterpiece of "Art." Clarissa herself has odd moments, early on in their cohabitation, when she seems half-conscious that he is victimizing her with interpretation—again, as in perhaps the saddest line in *Clarissa:* "I am but a *cypher*, to give *him* significance, and *myself* pain" (IV, 40)—but the full extent of his linguistic aggression remains invisible to her. (The real reader takes it on, of course, almost in her stead, in the Belford/ Lovelace correspondence.) Up to the crisis at Sinclair's, Clarissa remains for the most part an unwitting cipher, unaware of Lovelace's reading, unaware of that pleasure he takes in the text of her body itself.

Lovelace is supremely happy in his self-appointed role as Clarissa's exegete. In her, he finds the subject for his own compulsively manic discourse. "Indeed," he writes to Belford, "I never had a more illustrious subject to exercise my pen upon" (III, 26). Interestingly enough, Lovelace tends to merge the subject of interpretation with the political subject—again suggesting the fundamental link between them in the world of the novel. The bombastic imagery of conquest and empire, tyrants and subjects which he uses to encode his treatment of Clarissa points back to the more intimate, rhetorical subjugation going on in his letters themselves. Inverting the famous metaphor of Frantz Fanon, one might say that she is colonized by his writing.

Yet while Lovelace is busy circumscribing Clarissa's very body with the marks of "Woman"—the quintessentially empty sign of Western patriarchal discourse—he is also imposing similarly imaginative meanings on everything around her. His goal is domination; his means is systematic alteration of the systems of order through which she tries to understand herself and the world. He is conscious that Clarissa herself is an exegete, and that she is trying to interpret him too. After the arrival at Widow Sorling's, thus, he advises Belford contemptuously that Clarissa had best start plumbing his own behavior for meaning, as she might a text: "My Charmer has written to her Sister for her Cloaths, for some Gold, and for some of her Books. What Books can tell her more than she knows? But *I* can. So she had better study *me*" (III, 62). She "studies" him obviously, but without knowing the extent to which he shapes and exploits her reading of him, according to his plan. He is stunningly attuned to her interpretative naiveté, and her desire to disclose "Nature" behind the sign. Shunted about from place to place after the abduction, locked up finally at Sinclair's diabolical house, Clarissa travels with him across a map of misreading. She becomes increasingly unable to "make out" her duplicitous companion—a veritable "Proteus" of disguise and transformation, a magus who can alter at will the shape of what she sees. He is illegibility itself.

Clarissa's letters to Anna reflect the problem of reading.

What still more concerns me is, that every time I see this man, I am still at a greater loss than before what to make of him. I watch every turn of his countenance: And I think I see very deep lines in it. He looks with more meaning, I verily think, than he used to look; yet no more serious; not less gay—I don't know how he looks. [III, 25]

And soon, the language of interpretation itself begins to self-destruct, as the "subject" dissolves.

> I am strangely at a loss what to think of this man. He is a perfect Proteus. I can but write according to the shape he assumes at the time. Don't think *me* the changeable person, I beseech you, if in one Letter I contradict what I wrote in another; nay, if I seem to contradict what I said in the same Letter: For he is a perfect chameleon; or rather more variable than the chameleon; for that, it is said, cannot assume the *red* and the *white*; but this man *can*. And tho' *black* seems to be his natural colour, yet has he taken great pains to make me think him nothing but white. [III, 153-154]

The heroine's veering off into incoherence, paradox, contradiction, models the larger failure of her reading, the existential failure. With Lovelace, the world itself leaves her "strangely at a loss."

The hermeneutic confusion Clarissa experiences extends across a number of sign systems, including ultimately less obvious "languages" such as clothing and food. Primary focus falls, however, on the linguistic code itself. Language, spoken and written, is Lovelace's major manipulative tool, the most prominent weapon he deploys to achieve that *dérèglement de tous les sens* which is his goal with Clarissa. As we have already seen, she shows at times a distrust of her persecutor's words: she worries that he is in fact a "wicked Story-teller." But again, such is her faith in an absolute discourse of the "heart" that she is repeatedly caught out by what he says. Typically, Clarissa is implicated in the world of spoken and written language even at the moment she tries to disclaim it. Writing to Anna of her suspicions about Lovelace's speeches, she thus becomes pathetically tangled up in the linguistic circuit:

> I have not the better opinion of Mr. Lovelace for his extravagant volubility. He is too full of professions. He says too many fine things *of* me, and *to* me. True respect, true value, I think,

lies not in words: Words *cannot* express it: The silent awe, the humble, the doubting eye, and even the hesitating voice, better shew it by much, than, as our beloved Shakespeare says,

> —*The rattling tongue*
> *Of saucy and audacious eloquence.*
> [III, 23-24]

At the same time that Clarissa grants privileged status to the language of gesture (the voice, ideally, must only "hesitate"), her own utterance belies her point: she falls, schizophrenically, into citation, the appeal to words, to a textual "authority"—in this case Shakespeare. The Lovelacean appeal to literature contains a paradox about the heroine, of course, that a Lovelace would appreciate.

Clarissa's implacable escort plays upon this susceptibility. At all points before the rape, he floods her with promises and vows; he overwhelms her with language. As we discover in the Belford letters, these utterances are for Lovelace only "Lovers' *Oaths*," and "Do not the poets of two thousand years and upwards tell us, that Jupiter laughs at the perjuries of Lovers?" (V, 239). Vacuous speech, the "falsification of oaths, vows, and the like," is justified in one's dealings with women, Lovelace tells Belford, because the great conspiracy represented by the female sex itself demands it:

> Do not the Mothers, the Aunts, the Grandmothers, the Governesses of the pretty Innocents, always, from their very cradles to riper years, preach to them the deceitfulness of men? —That they are not to regard their oaths, vows, promises? —What a parcel of fibbers would all these reverend matrons be, if there were not now-and-then a pretty credulous rogue taken in for a justification of their preachments, and to serve as a beacon lighted up for the benefit of the rest. [V, 239]

Clarissa, in turn, believes every promise until it is proved false—which it invariably is. She trusts her own powers of "penetration," and thus each time she grants him "audience" she but prolongs and deepens her entanglement. Even when she thinks no one knows she is listening, she ends up being hypnotized, as it were, by Lovelace's unrestrained "professions." Early in the first period at Sinclair's, thus, Lovelace contrives for her to overhear a staged conversation between him and "the women below," in which he declares his love for her strictly of "*the true Platonick* kind" (IV, 151). Clarissa is immediately reassured. She acts here and elsewhere in terms of the banal proverbial *doxa* noted before by Lovelace's garrulous and idiotic uncle, Lord M.: "What everyone says, must be true" (IV, 126).

Clarissa is equally vulnerable to written words. When she demands a written marriage proposal from Lovelace and he makes her one, she assumes that he will be bound by it. What seems like foolishness on her part is in fact an impervious belief in the natural authority of documents, an almost superstitious assumption of their power to mirror human situations. What she reads *must* be true. Above all—and here one comes back upon the paradigmatic act of misreading taking place within the epistolary frame of *Clarissa*—Clarissa grants similarly unwarranted authority to letters themselves. She automatically naturalizes written correspondence. The letter, for her, is a transparent container for a certain *real* content; she lets it shape her view of reality. Clarissa's susceptibility to forgeries—as per the letters from Lovelace's "pretend relations" (actually him) and his faked letter to her, ostensibly from Anna Howe—is an extension of her general tendency to assign a "natural" point of origin to written discourse. She never questions the provenance of the letters she receives; the written artifact remains for her a pure communication, indissolubly linked by the "signature" to the body of the person she believes to have sent it. The possibility that letters can—and do—mediate falsely between persons, that they are open to interference and deformation, does not occur to her.

93

Perhaps the most telling example of the general syndrome is Clarissa's benighted response to the letter Lovelace receives at Widow Sorling's from "Mr. Doleman" (III, Letter 34), describing the several different London lodgings where Clarissa might safely reside. When Lovelace shows her the letter and lets her pick where she wants to stay, she chooses those in Dover-Street. She believes her choice a free one (she has watched Lovelace's reactions to her deliberations, and seen no sign of "visible preference" for any of the houses offered), but of course she has been set up. Her reading of the letter has been anticipated; indeed, its very rhetoric, it turns out, has been designed to incline her toward Dover-Street and Mrs. Sinclair. As we discover in Lovelace's own account of the exchange, the letter itself is not innocent; technically from Doleman, it has in fact been dictated by Lovelace himself, and Doleman is nothing other than his instrument. The farcically benevolent description of Sinclair's house, complete with former residents—"a *dignified Clergyman*, his *wife*, and *maiden-daughter*"—is Lovelace's invention, planned precisely to exploit Clarissa's gullibility. Nor does the pernicious effect of this particular document stop with Clarissa's choice: once she and Lovelace indeed arrive at Dover-Street, what Clarissa has already read in the letter about Sinclair and the house— that it is a boardinghouse for the genteel, and its owner the "reputable" "Relict" of a colonel—blinds her to the true nature of her surroundings. The letter, anterior to experience itself, afflicts her very perceptions. We go a long way toward explaining, therefore, Clarissa's seemingly imbecilic failure to realize (throughout the middle volumes of the novel) what sort of company she is really keeping when we relate her behavior to her career as a textual exegete. As Lovelace knows only too well, she believes what she reads. She is committed to what Lewis Mumford has called "the pseudo-environment of paper," where "what is visible and real . . . is only what has been transferred to paper"—that is, what has *already* been trans-

Denatured Signs

ferred to paper.[3] Underpinning this faith in the constraining power of the written artifact, again, are Clarissa's desire for meaning, and her naively inflated sense of herself as reader— as one who, in the act of interpretation, goes to the "heart" of the author's intention, to the core of truth itself. The letter imparts "Nature" to her. What she does not know yet, of course, is that letter and Nature both, like the rake, are heartless.

Clarissa's failure in the area of actual reading is once more, however, the literal counterpart to a deeper intellectual failure—an inability to decipher the surreal, estranging system of human relations in which, once she arrives at "Mother" Sinclair's, she becomes the central pathetic figure. Lovelace exploits her desire to comprehend words, spoken and written, as tokens of the actual; he likewise exploits her desire to comprehend human behavior itself. She is subjected to falsifications of every kind, to the unaccountable, alienating charades put on by her would-be paramour. She falls deeper into mystification. Despair and a sense of failing powers overtake her. She experiences, ultimately, a fragmentation of the self.

With Lovelace, first of all, linguistic abuse subtly modulates into a continuous suspension of conventional human identity. Once in London, "the only place in the world to be private in," Clarissa misreads the identity of virtually everyone she encounters. She is tricked by an elaborate series of impostors, all Lovelace's accomplices. But her disastrous entanglement with Sinclair, Tomlinson, and the rest is again a function of an absolutely uncritical mode of interpretation. Characteristically, Clarissa infers identity from a specific linguistic element—the proper name. She believes people are who they say they are, or who others say they are. Lovelace has no such stake in the names of persons. As he boasts to Belford, he is a

3. Lewis Mumford, *The Culture of Cities* (New York: Harcourt Brace, 1938), pp. 355–57; cited by Ian Watt, *The Rise of the Novel* (Berkeley: University of California Press, 1957), p. 196.

95

great "Name-Father." He knows that the names of objects and persons, like all linguistic signs, are conventional markers, grounded in ordinary usage, but without *essential* relation to the things they name. They can be separated from their usual referents and affixed at random elsewhere. To switch names around is to rearrange reality; by rewriting the proper name (through an act of "authority") one rewrites human identity. Speaking of one of his naming-plots, thus, Lovelace expands upon this form of semantic imperialism:

> I have changed his name by virtue of my own single authority. Knowest thou not, that I am a great Name-Father? Preferments I bestow, both military and civil. I give Estates, and take them away at my pleasure. Quality too I create. And by a still more valuable prerogative, I *degrade* by virtue of my own imperial will, without any other act of forfeiture than for my own convenience. What a poor thing is a monarch to me! [IV, 44]

Lovelace uses the inherent instability of the name to play havoc with Clarissa's sense both of who *she* is, and who other people are. Early on, for example, she finds her own identity, confusingly enough, revised by his naming. At Sorling's, she becomes his "sister" for a time; at Sinclair's, she becomes his betrothed, "Mrs. Lovelace." Clarissa is profoundly troubled by these linguistic transformations, for as well as suggesting a greater intimacy with Lovelace than she is prepared to accept, they affront her assumptions about the relation between language and reality. Ironically, however—in this world of endless hermeneutic violence—she is powerless to stop Lovelace from fictionalizing her identity without opening herself once again, as she says, to "construction": the odious interpretations of her behavior which she believes other people will make if they discover she is not indeed related to her escort at all.

The fact that Lovelace produces a new meaning, in effect,

for Clarissa's own person—making her over into a "Lovelace" on several occasions—does not alert her to the possibility that he is making similar transformations elsewhere. The byzantine game of impersonation he sets in motion relies, of course, upon an identical alienation of the linguistic token, the proper name, away from its ostensible referent. She is victimized by charlatans, beginning with "Mrs. Sinclair" herself, the "old Relict" whose phony name is in fact Lovelace's appalling inside-out joke on Clarissa's own. The actual identity of the woman running the house on Dover Street is never made clear in *Clarissa*, even in Lovelace's letters: "Ay, SINCLAIR, Jack!— Remember the name! SINCLAIR, I repeat. She *has* no other" (III, 201). This is a point on which the real reader's ignorance remains as great as Clarissa's. Other fakes follow: "Tomlinson" (a.k.a., Patrick MacDonald), "Mr. Mennell" (Newcomb), "Singleton's mate" (Paul Wheatley), and Lovelace's "pretend relations," "Miss Montague" and "Lady Betty" (Bab. Wallis and Johanetta Golding). At times the name can be without any body behind it at all—even a false body—as in the case of "Mrs. Fretchville," the imaginary lady with smallpox whose house Clarissa is led to believe she and Lovelace will let after their marriage. Clarissa is caught, thus, in a world where the links between names and individuals are artificial and profoundly variable. Personal identity itself is a construct—a function of language alone, a matter of conventional usage. Patrick MacDonald becomes "Captain Tomlinson" because that is what Lovelace and the "women below" call him: Clarissa accepts their referential mode, and all its implications, without considering its ontological basis (or lack thereof). Clarissa's disastrous error, as always, is that she believes she understands how signs signify. She is a nominalist in a world where such faith is folly. She interprets name as "Nature." She weds it to being itself, human essence. The fictions of the "Name-Father" rupture this naturalized bond, however, and substitute fables of identity for identity itself.

Clarissa is made the gull of all his "unnatural" acquaintances, the set of vile bodies who surround her, converge on her, hold her prisoner.

The world into which Lovelace initiates Clarissa is denatured in still other aspects. Everything in it is in fact a triumph of "Art." As at Harlowe-Place, the heroine's conventional models of behavior, like her models of linguistic usage, are insufficient to the interpretation of its vagaries. For all her "watchful penetration" (Lovelace speaks at several points in mock fear of her "penetrating eye"), she is the dupe of appearances—of phenomenological data as much as of words. She reads natural meaning into physical symptoms, where, as before, it does not exist. From our privileged position outside the fiction (in dubious possession too of Lovelace's own metacriticism on the text of Clarissa), we follow painfully this process of misreading. In the complex phenomenological domain over which Lovelace so gaily reigns, Clarissa's innocent pursuit of meaning is finally tragically compromising.

The infamous house on Dover-Street is a demonic microcosm of the topsy-turvy fictional world—and the morbid arena for Lovelace's most outrageous semantic manipulations. "Mother" Sinclair stands as the central emblem of this pervasive phenomenological instability: her apparent "Nature" and her actual function in regard to the heroine are at odds. She embodies the disordering of naturalized human relations; she inverts, and perverts, conventional codes of meaning. The familial and sexual functions suggested by her nickname—the associations of "motherhood"—have no bearing upon her behavior. Sinclair is neither maternal, nor apparently even feminine in any stereotypical sense. On the first count, she is a more nightmarish version of Mrs. Harlowe, the original non-mothering mother in *Clarissa*. The relation between "Mother" Sinclair and "daughter" Clarissa is one founded not in "tenderness" (Clarissa's catchword for maternal feeling), but in brutality, with hints also of an incestuous kind of sexuality. (Later, damningly, Sinclair's "milk" will turn out to be bad, the opposite of nourishment—it is that loathesome "London milk" with which Clarissa is drugged, prior to her sexual usage by Lovelace and the "women below," including Sinclair herself.) Likewise, her sex itself is disturbingly ambiguous: she has "a *masculine air*," and is "a *little forbidding at first*" (III, 195).

"Masculine" Sinclair's breaching of conventional sexual boundaries, it should be noted, seems to be linked to a similar tendency in Lovelace himself. On several occasions, for example, while ostensibly plotting ways of getting closer to the object of his desire, he fantasizes disguising himself as a woman, or else in the "effeminate" robes of a clergyman. The wish for a mutation of gender suggested by the transvestite fantasy becomes a reality (of sorts) in his amazing dream, early in Volume VI, where he is incarnated as the old bawd "Mother H." In his female form, Lovelace kidnaps the heroine in the street, takes her to obscure lodgings, and in a scene charged with lesbian eroticism, sleeps with her in the same bed in order "to hear more of the young Lady's Story." It is only near the end of this "strange promiscuous huddle of adventures" that Lovelace resumes his masculinity. "What unaccountable things," he writes, "are dreams!" (VI, 12).

The hints of sexual variance in Sinclair point again to an essential arbitrariness at the heart of things in the fictional world: biological sex does not determine behavior; indeed the conventional behavioral distinctions between the sexes can be overturned by individuals, like Sinclair, who symbolize mediation between, or confusion of sexual categories.[4] Confronting this hallucinatory figure who contradicts her ways of assigning meaning to familial and gender relationships, Clarissa, for her part, is perplexed, disoriented, even paralyzed by the ambiguities of the situation. She "likes not greatly" and suspects the "Widow" from the start, but cannot sort out exactly what

4. See Judith Wilt's treatment of Mrs. Sinclair's "masculine" functions in "He Could Go No Farther: A Modest Proposal About Lovelace and Clarissa," *PMLA*, 92 (1977), 27.

is wrong. She is not attuned, obviously, to the irony that permeates Lovelace's view of "our dear Mother," nor to the campy role playing of the "old Relict" herself. Later, of course—but much later—perplexity will turn to terrifying awareness of Sinclair's evil, when, in the moments before the rape, "Mother Damnable," the "vilest of vile women," is brought before Clarissa to frighten her with "masculine violence." "Never was there so horrible a creature as she appeared to me at the time" (VI, 190). But until then, catastrophically, Clarissa persists in an attempt to naturalize this most unnatural of figures, to act toward Sinclair as though she were indeed what she is supposed to be—woman, widow, mother. Clarissa acts thus even while Sinclair's presence boggles meaning itself, and renders useless her accustomed ways of knowing.

If Clarissa does not know how to gloss Mrs. Sinclair, she is likewise the victim of other contradictory, and apparently nonsensical texts on display at the London house. She is duped by human phenomena at the very moment she strains to decipher in them a natural significance. The world of her imprisonment is one, for example, in which the visual sign systems through which individuals communicate, like the code of language itself, reveal themselves as denatured, arbitrary, and hence open to exploitation. Normally significant secondary human languages—the sartorial code, the system of physical gestures, street signs, even minor semiotic systems like the language of heraldic markings—undergo disruption, and yield up deceptive messages. The situation is not unlike that which Ronald Paulson has described operating in some of Hogarth's prints: the iconographic signs Clarissa encounters are ambiguous, polysemous.[5] The visual field itself throws into question her simplified way of reading the world.

5. Ronald Paulson, *Emblem and Expression: Meaning in English Art in the Eighteenth Century* (Cambridge, Mass.: Harvard University Press, 1975).

The physical realm through which Clarissa passes is one in which meaningful markers are either absent altogether or utterly misleading. The book of the world is at once elliptical and layered with multiple significance. Among absent signs, thus, are all those which would allow Clarissa to identify her real surroundings. The London house is unmarked: she believes herself to be on Dover-Street (and indeed, I have referred to Sinclair's brothel as "the house on Dover-Street"), but, as Lovelace tells Belford in a letter, that is not where she really is at all. The actual location of Sinclair's house remains unknown. The heroine's captor exults that even if one located Dover-Street on a map, one would still not locate the place itself: "Suppose the *widow Sinclair's in Dover-Street* should be enquired after by some officious person . . . ; and neither such a name, nor such a house, can be found in that Street, nor a house to answer the description; then will not the keenest hunter in England be at fault?" (III, 200). One might call Lovelace's tactic here a disruption of the topographic, or even cartographic code of meaning: his artifices rob the map of its conventional signifying function. There is apparently nothing in Clarissa's immediate surroundings, nothing on the house itself, nothing in the view from her "closet" of adjacent buildings, to let her know her true location. Sinclair's "boarding-house" itself is a cipher, lacking any identifying outward symbol, even though other buildings in *Clarissa* (notably Smith's) carry signboards that indicate their functions. Clarissa, not surprisingly, seems blind to these gaps in the signifying system; her sense of where she is has already been conditioned by language, by Lovelace telling her they are in fact on Dover-Street. She sees nothing in her environs to contradict this; unfortunately, she sees nothing to confirm it either.

Lovelace exploits Clarissa's obliviousness to missing signs again, of course. In the crucial scene in which his "pretend-relations," the false Lady Betty and Miss Montague, come to Mrs. Moore's to take Clarissa away to the family estate and safety, the impostors travel in a coach that does not bear the customary heraldic devices. They explain this absence by saying their usual coach is being "cleaned" and that they have hired a substitute. In some sense the explanation is unnecessary, however, because Clarissa, once more, seems to read nothing into the absence of the Lovelace "Lozenge," even though the lack itself is perversely meaningful: it undermines utterly the ladies' aristocratic pretense. Similarly, Clarissa later fails to recognize one of Lovelace's servants because Lovelace has replaced the man's distinctive livery with nondescript dress. Distinguishing marks, drawn from conventional contemporary systems of visual syntax, are thus frequently oddly absent in *Clarissa*; and the heroine, the would-be exegete, is victimized precisely by such lacunae.

In addition to failing to notice missing signs, Clarissa is deceived by those visual systems that only appear to hold out meanings. Among the systems manipulated thus by her dapper trickster-consort, the code of fashion, not surprisingly, figures prominently. Lovelace is obsessed with clothing, apparently to a fetishistic degree (viz., his fantasia on Clarissa's "pale primrose-coloured paduasoy" morning gown, "blue satten" shoes, "black velvet glove-like muffs," etc., in Volume III, Letter 3). But so too is the heroine. Along with everything else, Clarissa naturalizes dress—the signifying functions attached to clothing, what Barthes would call the *systéme de la mode*. Borrowing Anne Hollander's wordplay, one could say that Clarissa "sees through clothes"; she interprets them. But again the process of interpretation is innocent: Clarissa views dress as a transparent index to the "nature" of the person wearing it, as outward sign of actual social status, profession, age, gender, morals, and so on. Her trust in the pure significance of garments is linked to her faith in language itself. In a letter to Anna, she alludes to the famous commonplace of eighteenth-century aesthetics (language is the dress of thought) which specifically figures linguistic truth in terms of the signifying power of clothing. Clarissa makes the metaphoric point explicit: both the linguistic and the sartorial code convey obvious and accessible meanings: "For what are *words*, but the *body* and *dress* of *thought?* And is not the mind of a person strongly indicated by outward dress?" (III, 365). "Mind," the inner life, once again, is available to the reader of clothing.

Lovelace, in contrast, is obsessed with dress as costume—as disguise for, rather than revelation of the inner person. Thus he fools Clarissa again and again by exploiting the simple fact that clothes do *not* communicate naturally, that sartorial signs are as unconstrained as any other. One may wear anything, and thereby alter the message one's person conveys.

Lovelace disguises both himself and others. Clarissa believes that the individual dressed as an old man who visits her at Hampstead after the escape to Mrs. Moore's *is* an old man, though it is Lovelace, "muffled up" like "an antiquated beau" (V, 79). Likewise, she invariably thinks women dressed as "ladies of fashion" are indeed ladies of fashion, when in fact they are Lovelace's tarts, togged up to delude her. (Lovelace's account of how he disguises the "flaming" "Prisc. Partington" to look like a demure young gentlewoman so she can come to the card party he is arranging for Clarissa represents one of his standard sartorial impertinences.) Similarly, Clarissa is for a long time confused by the fact that under normal circumstances Lovelace dresses "soberly." Belford—much less the true rake—typically wears foppish attire. On the basis of the clothing system alone, Clarissa is thus inclined, right up to the moment of betrayal, to give Lovelace more than his due, and Belford less than his. Lovelace himself is aware of the semiotic paradox here. Writing to his friend, he notes that "a Fop . . . takes great pains to hang out a Sign by his dress of what he has in his Shop. Thou, indeed, art an exception; dressing like a Coxcomb, yet a very clever fellow" (VI, 394). The heroine's interpretative problem is shared by the real reader. The fact that Belford—who increasingly becomes our moral guide through the later part of the fiction, and takes on all the other accoutrements, ethical and spiritual, of the "Reformed Rake"—persists in tasteless attire, while Lovelace's clothes remain impeccable and nonrakish suggests a deep irregularity in the structure of meaning ostensibly underlying Richardson's fiction. Antithetical symbolism repeatedly attaches itself to main characters in *Clarissa*, even as their moral natures are supposedly being clarified. Thus for the real reader the problem of assigning fixed meaning to the text itself is perpetually reintroduced.

The prevalence of disguise in *Clarissa*, fashion as artifice—the estrangement of the sartorial code from any "Nature"—points finally to a larger system of "bad Signs" involving the human body itself. Just as at the Harlowes' earlier, where "countenance," gesture, physical reactions—all the signifying activities of the body per se—were measured, alienated, and ultimately ambiguous, so the language of the body that Clarissa confronts at Dover-Street is similarly treacherous. Mrs. Sinclair's feigned deference to the heroine is typical. Lovelace describes for Belford (and for the real reader) her sham "puritanical behaviour":

> Not an oath, not a curse, nor the least free word, escapes her lips. She minces in her gaite. She prims up her horse-mouth. Her voice, which when she pleases, is the voice of thunder, is sunk into an humble whine. Her stiff hams, that have not been bent to a civility for ten years past, are now limbered into courtesies three-deep at every word. Her fat arms are crossed before her; and she can hardly be prevailed to sit in the presence of my goddess. [III, 348]

Clarissa here, as before, is still utterly vulnerable, even to such patently false gestures as Sinclair's. She clings, hope against hope, to a faith in her own powers of interpretation, her own ability to decipher the discourse of the body itself—

paradoxically, the most natural-seeming of all human signifying systems. She clings to this faith particularly in regard to
Lovelace himself. Her descriptions of him reveal at once her
hermeneutic mania and her hermeneutic folly. One such
gloss—in which she tries vainly to sort out what is "natural" in
Lovelace's person and what artificial—verges on the schizoid:

> It must, indeed, be confessed, that there is in his whole de-
> portment a natural dignity, which renders all insolent or im-
> perative demeanour as unnecessary as inexcusable. Then that
> deceiving sweetness which appears in his smiles, in his accent,
> in his whole aspect and address, when he thinks it worth his
> while to oblige, or endeavour to attract, how does this shew,
> that he was *born* innocent, as I may say; that he was not
> *naturally* the cruel, the boisterous, the impetuous creature,
> which the wicked company he may have fallen into have made
> him! For he has, besides, an open, and, I think, an honest
> countenance. Don't *you* think so, my dear? —On all these
> specious appearances, have I founded my hopes of seeing him a
> reformed man. [III, 370-71]

The peculiarly convoluted appeal to Lovelace's natural innocence, besides suggesting that Clarissa may have misread
Christian doctrine on a crucial point, is characteristic: Clarissa
believes she can read the signs of truth on the body itself.

But even the body somehow passes out of the realm of
"Nature" in *Clarissa,* and into the realm of "Art." Basic
physiological responses—the whole range of organic
symptoms—are subsumed by Lovelace's great passionate fictions. The infamous "Ipecac-trick" for instance, is an alarming
demonstration of the syndrome. In an almost crazy display of
obsessiveness, Lovelace, we recall, takes ipecacuanha in order
to feign sickness and thereby test Clarissa's feeling for him.
Will she show concern for him if he is ill? (Lovelace, one must
add, is typically ready to reinterpret any compassion on her
part as subliminal sexual desire.) Innocent diagnostician that

she is, Clarissa indeed responds sympathetically: she assumes the "natural" symptoms—retching, weakness, pain—point back to an organic source. Here Clarissa interprets according to a kind of metonymy of the body: the visible symptom is the outward sign of hidden pathology, an index to the underlying physical disorder. Lovelace's ploy, however, revokes the semantic rule of the body itself, and substitutes an artificial cause for the organic disturbance. The interruption and suspension of the "natural" signifying chain is thus radical, complete.

The "Ipecac-trick" resonates weirdly, of course, with other hermeneutic dislocations occurring later in *Clarissa*. Lovelace's artificially motivated illness—he is at once sick and not sick—prefigures Clarissa's own wasting disease after the rape, which is similarly indeterminate in origin, and possibly alienated from organic causes. The reader's determination regarding the heroine's pathology—what do we decide *is* the cause of her death?—recapitulates Clarissa's own implicit act of interpretation (diagnosis) in regard to Lovelace. The Ipecac-trick likewise introduces the important motif of ingestion, and suggests the denatured status of the "code of food" in the fiction. Lovelace's tasting of the ipecac—an ostensibly unnatural form of nourishment—is echoed later in Clarissa's ingestion of a similarly denatured food, the uncanny drugged tea, with its dose of "London milk." In the world of *Clarissa*, conventional distinctions between what is edible and what is not repeatedly dissolve. Clarissa consumes the "inedible" in the drugging scene (through an error of interpretation), and later, after her violation and escape, refuses the "edible" in favor of spiritual nourishment. The upshot of all of this—oddly reminiscent of Claude Lévi-Strauss's demystification of alimentary codes in *The Raw and the Cooked*—is the suspension of our sense of an absolute standard of edibility. Anything may be interpreted (or not interpreted) as "food." The distinction between what may be eaten and what may not does not depend upon any biological criterion—Clarissa's "Nature"—but seems an arbitrary function, a matter of social contingency. Given the tragic mode of the fiction, the chaos in the alimentary system has disastrous effects: Clarissa's interpretation of Mrs. Sinclair's odious tea as edible substance results, indirectly, in her violation. It is thus related to her ongoing, misguided, and finally compromising attempt to *digest* the incomprehensible details of the world in which she is caught.

The life of the body in *Clarissa*, therefore, is itself an inscription of sorts—and the physical symptom nothing more than a "construction," a meaning-effect. The Ipecac-trick is perhaps the most sinister early example of the kind of estrangement Lovelace effects between physical signs and "Nature," but it is characteristic of his stratagems elsewhere. Here and everywhere, he presents his own body as a text for Clarissa's beguiled perusal.

6

The Voyage Out

The despicable, endlessly idiotic, endlessly suggestive act upon which *histoire* in *Clarissa* turns—the rape of the heroine—is deeply tied in to the hermeneutic theme. Sexual violation, the "black transaction" at the heart of the fiction, is at once the consequence and emblem of Clarissa's tragic misreadings, and of all the "constructions" with which she has been circumscribed. A kind of demented fatality leads Lovelace from hermeneutic violence against her to actual sexual violence: his very literal infiltration of Clarissa's body is intimately related to that infiltration of sign systems he has already effected in order to control her. Rape is the culminating interruption in a long pattern of interference and intrusion, a climax in the drama of "penetration" to which he has subjected her.

Paradoxically, this brutality, which in a sense concludes Lovelace's histrionic reading of Clarissa as "Woman" (he can "go no farther"), provides her with a ground for action, a ground for escape. Before, she succeeds briefly in escaping physically from Lovelace—with the flight to Mrs. Moore's at Hampstead—but her liberation is incomplete; she is still implicated in the world of interpretation (the world of the letter, the world of the fiction). Lovelace soon catches her out again, by exploiting her still insistent desire for meaning. He sets new texts for her to decipher, and she falls back into his hands—inevitably, poignantly. Ironically, true escape begins with violation.

Thus commentators on *Clarissa* note often that after the rape Lovelace finds Clarissa's "will" suddenly and curiously activated. When all his plots come to light, she takes on, at last, an "authority," an outrage, that he has never seen in her before. Rather than confirming her humiliation, the experience of rape energizes new powers of psychic resistance. She henceforth despises Lovelace—with a kind of magnificent lucidity. A successful physical flight soon follows.[1] Yet what has often been called Clarissa's "moral" escape has another dimension. Through an extended and complex process of disaffiliation, she leaves behind the gibbering, incoherent world of "bad Signs" itself. Reading has led to a calamity of the body; the body, at this point, escapes the world of reading. Clarissa's physical trauma is epiphanic: it makes her conscious, as nothing else has done, of the politics of meaning in which she has been caught, the insufficiency of her own readings, and the basic, terrifying absence of "Nature" itself from human exchanges. The myth of the "dictating heart" simultaneously collapses. Clarissa's celebrated "long time a-dying" becomes, thus, a methodical self-expulsion from the realm of signification. She disaffects herself; she ceases to read. The act also closes down the fiction that bears her name: in the epistolary format, the flight from reading—from participation in that system of transaction represented by the letter—is always equivalent to death. Clarissa ceases to "corre-, spond" in any sense; the event figures her demise. Likewise, as soon as she disappears from the great epistolary chain, *Clarissa* itself enters its death throes.

1. Elizabeth R. Napier. "'Tremble and Reform': The Inversion of Power in Richardson's *Clarissa*," *ELH*, 42 (1975), 214-23.

In the events immediately preceding Clarissa's sexual "usage," all the motifs associated with reading and interpretation reappear in condensed form. Clarissa's sexual vulnerability extends out of a welter of interrelated misreadings that occur across all those signifying systems we have seen. On the level of actual reading, to start with, Clarissa's fall is precipitated by Lovelace's crucial forgery of Anna Howe's writing (v, Letter 14), the false letter he sends after intercepting Anna's real one warning the heroine of his plots. Lovelace fragments Anna's text—cutting out the parts that incriminate him, adding little misleading bits of his own, and appending finally a fictional postscript to allay suspicion regarding the authenticity of the document ("Excuse indifferent writing. My crow quills are worn to the stump, and I must get a new supply" [v, 172]). Clarissa typically does not question the letter's provenance, and is set up for recapture. When Lovelace finds her again at Mrs. Moore's, hermeneutic manipulation spreads to other levels. Lovelace at first uses physical disguise to gain access to her, and soon after brings on Tomlinson, the false messenger from Uncle Harlowe, in order to lull Clarissa into optimism regarding the marriage proposals and the possibility of reconciliation with her family. At the tragicomic interview between the three of them, Lovelace, stage-managing, characteristically delights in creating secret messages that utterly bypass the heroine. He signals to Tomlinson in a private code of gestures invented ahead of time: a ludicrous artificial language composed of nods and becks and mugging.

As thus [he writes]—A wink of the left-eye was to signify *Push that point, Captain*.

A wink of the right, and a nod, was to indicate *Approbation* of what he had said.

My forefinger held up, and biting my lip, *Get off of that, as fast as possible*.

A right-forward nod, and a frown—*Swear to it, Captain*.

My whole spread hand, *To take care not to say too much on that particular subject.*

A scouling brow, and a positive nod, was to bid him *rise in his temper.* [v, 208–209]

Lovelace concludes his charades, finally, by presenting Clarissa with the "pretend-relations," decked out with false names, false clothes, and a false coach. "True *Spartan* dames" these are—"ashamed of nothing but *detection*—Always, there-fore, upon their guard against that. And in their own conceit, when assuming top parts, the very Quality they ape" (v, 298). Once more Clarissa accepts the challenge to her exegetical skill, and interprets with that devastating naiveté characteristic of her. Even when the coach pulls up at Mrs. Sinclair's instead of "Cousin Leeson's," Clarissa, as she will explain to Anna much later, still does not "suspect these women." "I little thought that there could be such impostors in the world" (vi, 166). Once at Sinclair's, she is again subjected to empty words from Lovelace. Swearing that their stay there will only be a short one, he resumes his manic "professions." He tells Bel-ford later: "Revowed all my old vows and poured forth new ones" (v, 309). Clarissa's confused and anguished response—reminiscent of her demoralization at Harlowe-Place—is a paradigm of broken utterance. She can only reply to Lovelace and his minions with "broken sentences" and a "heart-breaking sob." Her head sinks, finally, "like a half-broken-stalked Lilly, top-heavy with the over-charging dews of the morning" (v, 310).

Clarissa's physical violation is another "breakage," of course. She is "penetrated"; and the text of her body itself opened to Lovelace's phallic gloss. He annotates her; he frag-ments her. Once again, the textual metaphor is inescapable, and suggests the pervasive merging in *Clarissa*, on the phan-tasmic level, of written artifact and the heroine's body. Lovelace's own strangely eroticized use of textual devices en-

forces the distressing connection. When he intercepts the vital
warning letter from Anna Howe to Clarissa, for instance, he
sends Belford a copy (which the real reader also sees), marked
up, indeed violated, by obsessive traces of his own "reading."
The text of the letter (v, Letter 4) is "crouded with indices"
[☞]—a myriad of tiny hands in the margin which point to
remarks made by Anna which Lovelace finds particularly en-
raging. For the real reader, the effect of the hands is fetishistic,
oppressive, disturbing (see Figure 1). The hands, first, are
little images of dismemberment, and thus related to other real
or threatened physical amputations taking place in *Clarissa*—
Sinclair's "half-mortified Femur" being the paradigm. But
their primary visual significance seems to be that they are
suggestive, potential inserts into the *body* of the letter itself.
They press in upon the text; they threaten to break it up—
literally. Lovelace's use of the index invites, of course, a
psychoanalytic gloss—as orthographic representation of the
intruding phallus, according to the Freudian model of the
displacement upward.[2] But the point seems clear enough,
even without any explicit Freudian apparatus: Lovelace's impulse toward fragmentation, toward interruption of surfaces,
easily extends from one system to the other—from "penetration" of the text (exegesis) to sexual penetration (rape). One
may not like it, but the hands-letter has, finally, something of
the silly redundancy of a bad dream: as when Anna warns the
heroine—*in* the disrupted letter itself—"[You are] in his
hands" (v, 39). The unconstrained typographic repetition of

2. See the famous passage in *The Interpretation of Dreams* in which Freud,
analyzing a dream about teeth, introduces the concept of "displacement
from below to above"—that operation "which is at the service of sexual
repression, and by means of which all kinds of sensations and intentions
occurring in hysteria, which ought to be localized in the genitals, may at all
events be realized in other, unobjectionable parts of the body." Freud, *The
Interpretation of Dreams*, in *The Basic Writings of Sigmund Freud*, ed. A. A. Brill
(New York: The Modern Library, 1938), p. 388.

brought you to, to be a vile one. This is a clue that has
led me to account for all his behaviour to you ever since
you have been in his hands.

Allow me a brief retrospection of it all.

We both know, that Pride, Revenge, and a delight to
tread in unbeaten paths, are principal ingredients in the
character of this finished Libertine.

☞ He hates all your family, yourself excepted; and I have
several times thought, that I have seen him stung and
mortified that Love has obliged him to kneel at your
☞footstool, because you are a *Harlowe*.—Yet is this wretch
a Savage in Love.—Love that humanizes the fiercest
☞spirits, has not been able to subdue his. His *Pride*, and
☞the credit which a few *plausible qualities*, sprinkled among
his *odious ones*, have given him, have secured him too
good a reception from our eye-judging, our undisting-
uishing, our self-flattering, our too-confiding Sex, to
make assiduity and obsequiousness, and a conquest of his
unruly passions, any part of his study.

☞ He has some reason for his animosity to *all* the men,
and to *one* woman of your family. He has always shewn
☞you, and his own family too, that he prefers his Pride to
his Interest. He is a declared Marriage-hater: A notorious Intriguer: Full of his inventions; and glorying in
them.—He never could draw you into declarations of
Love: Nor, till your *wise* relations persecuted you, as
☞they did, to receive his addresses as a Lover.—He knew,
that you professedly disliked him for his immoralities;
he could not therefore justly blame you for the coldness
and indifference of your behaviour to him.

☞ The prevention of mischief was your first main view
in the correspondence he drew you into. He ought not,
then, to have wondered, that you declared your prefer-

FIGURE 1. Lovelace's indices to Anna's letter to Clarissa ("you have been
in his hands"). From the Shakespeare Head Press edition of *Clarissa* (Oxford: Basil Blackwell, 1943).

Lovelace's inane little digits in turn serves to prod us, the real readers, toward the symbolic implication.

Lovelace's sexual aggression follows with perfect consistency upon his reading of Clarissa as "Woman." "Rapes, vulgarly so called," he writes, but confirm Woman's corrupt, secret sexuality: female "Virtue" is "owing to Education only," and once lost soon forgotten (v, 145). By refusing intimacy with him, Clarissa but demonstrates the hypocritical vanity of her sex, who demur in order to excite. "Yet is she not a woman?" he asks Belford (IV, 238). "And should not my Beloved, for her own sake, descend, by *degrees*, from *Goddesshood* into *Humanity*? If it be *Pride* that restrains her, ought not that pride to be punished?" (IV, 354-55). Again, railing: "Don't tell me, that Virtue and Principle are her guides on this occasion! —'Tis *Pride*, a greater Pride than my own, that governs her. . . . She cannot bear to be thought a *woman*, I warrant!" (v, 284). Rape is the final arbitrary turn in his great argument. When Clarissa yields to his "nightly surprizes," as he assumes she will, his interpretation of her nature will be definitively enacted. The event but solidifies that thesis already written and rewritten in his imagination—the fantasy constructed by desire. Sexual violence, one might say, is thus a form of articulation for Lovelace. It conveys as nothing else could his reading—always pathological and banal—of Clarissa's essence.

For the woman, however, the act of rape is otherwise. Significantly—particularly in light of that motif of interruption associated with Clarissa throughout the fiction—it marks off a death of articulation, a death of reading. Clarissa's ordeal begins with a kind of oral interference, a stopping up of her mouth, when she is forced by the "women below" to take in Mrs. Sinclair's diabolical tea, which when she swallows it only makes her more thirsty. She loses her "intellects" as a result of the "stupefying potions," and Lovelace has his way while she is in a state of dumb "senselessness." The filling up of Clarissa's mouth not only recollects her treatment at the hands of Arabella and Mrs. Harlowe, who stuff things in her mouth to keep her from speaking; it prefigures the now imminent filling up of another orifice, the vaginal "mouth," in the moment of rape itself. Simultaneously penetrated above and below, the heroine is robbed of utterance. A subject of the "usage" of others, she herself passes out of the realm of speech, the realm of protest. She suffers a little death, an involuntary muting.

Clarissa's rape is a primal act of silencing. By stratagem, by force, the flow of her speech is stopped. The fiction itself undergoes a kind of aphasia at the same time as the heroine: after Lovelace's infamous "I can go no farther" note to Belford, all details of the actual penetration are censored. The text becomes uncommunicative; the real reader experiences a gap in the information—rendered typographically by those solid black lines that disrupt the epistolary sequence at the moment of violation (v, 314). The Editor's announcement that "*the whole of this black transaction*" will be described later in Clarissa's letters in Vol. vi covers over, thus, a hole in the text. Yet this very literal interruption of Clarissa's articulation is also a summarizing image of the hermeneutic distress she has everywhere been made to suffer. Lovelace's act of violence is an ultimate demonstration of the violence inherent in reading itself.

In the profoundest sense, the rape of Clarissa is a form of hermeneutic intimidation. It is, one might say, a punishment for attempting to interpret and express in her own way—with terms supplied by "Nature." Throughout the fiction, as we have seen, Clarissa's efforts to make sense of her experience— to read, in the greater existential sense—have been frustrated and parodied, by her family and by Lovelace himself. She has been subject to the aggression of those who have imposed their own readings upon her, arbitrarily; she has seen her own analysis of experience suspended, overturned, negated. The act of rape projects, on the intimate plane of the body, this basic loss of power. Physical violence is the final devastating proof of Clarissa's lack of "authority." She knows not, indeed, what true authority is. As child, as woman, she has read in terms of "Nature," unaware that such interpretations carry no compulsion in the world of "Art." She is open to abuse precisely because her trust in the nature of things has been too great, and she has wanted too much—at least in the eyes of the Harlowes and Lovelace—to testify to her trust.

But Lovelace's ultimate gesture of "force" (as he calls it) exposes a truth about meaning itself. The power to determine the significance of events, to articulate one's reading of experience and impose it on others, is a function of political advantage alone, and identified finally with physical force. The person who prevails in the unconstrained fictional world is one who supports his "construction," as Lovelace does, with an implicit power to do violence to others. The great book of phenomena supplies no meanings; the text itself is only a human inscription, and a function of aggression.

As a number of critics have already noted, the power relationship between Lovelace and Clarissa invites feminist commentary. Indeed, it is clear, I hope, that the hermeneutic theme we have been following here can easily be given a historical and sociological expansion in just such terms. Clarissa's powerlessness, figured first as exclusion from realms of articulation (a loss equivalent finally to the lack of freedom to tell her own "Story" or interpret the world on her own terms) models in little a historical condition of women in patriarchal cultures. Her linguistic oppression is linked to other sorts of oppression: economic, social, psychological—and most basically—vulnerability to physical abuse, archetypally confirmed in the ancient violence of rape itself. The crucial importance of violation in Clarissa's history is not that it has so much to do with an isolated and sentimentalized theme of female "Virtue," but that it points to a larger, multileveled pattern of sexual and political exploitation. For Lovelace, rape is trivial, that "cause

so common, and so slight" (v, 325)—a view unfortunately
shared by a number of commentators on Richardson's fiction.[3]
But though sexual violence may be common in the "old Patriarchal system" (again Lovelace's words), it is never slight: as
Susan Brownmiller has suggested, rape in fact implicitly
underpins patriarchal society because it at once asserts and
enforces—on all levels—the ideology of male supremacy.[4]
The quintessential act of violence against women, it is that
hidden physical threat held over the woman who tries, wit-
tingly or unwittingly, to overstep any of the fundamental re-
strictions on her power—in any arena. Within the feminist
critical model, therefore, Clarissa's punishment is eminently
predictable. Given the displacement of power in patriarchal
culture—the culture in which she and Lovelace collide—her
attempt to voice the self through the act of interpretation
results inevitably in a great silencing.

Clarissa's steady loss of control over her own physical integrity, a loss culminating classically in rape, marks off, then, a
hermeneutic defeat. As Lovelace acts out on her his own
triumphant reading, she is herself "cut off" from the possibility of reading. Her own "heartfelt" inscription of the world,
the fragmentary and poignant interpretation of things which

3. Ironically it is a woman, Dorothy Van Ghent, who has written most
dismissively of Clarissa's rape. In *The English Novel: Form and Function* (New
York: Holt, Rinehart, & Winston, 1953) she described it as "a singularly
thin and unrewarding piece of action" (p. 47). Her casualness on the matter,
though not at all surprising for a woman critic writing in 1953, is still
disturbing because it has so often been echoed rather than challenged by
later critics. As Judith Wilt points out, Van Ghent's embarrassingly rapid
elision over the subject of sexual violation makes it impossible to concur with
that "popular judgment, expressed most recently by Phillip Stevick (introd.
to *Clarissa*, New York: Rinehart, 1971), that [hers] is really the only piece of
criticism one need read on *Clarissa*" (Wilt, "He Could Go No Farther: A
Modest Proposal About Lovelace and Clarissa," *PMLA*, 92 [1977], p. 32, n.
1).
4. Susan Brownmiller, *Against Our Will: Men, Women, and Rape* (New
York: Simon & Schuster, 1975). See in particular chapters 1 and 2, "The
Mass Psychology of Rape" and "In the Beginning was the Law."

she has tried to produce, and which we have seen replicated in her damaged and disrupted correspondence, is erased entirely.

And after this "interruption," Clarissa of course slips away. Brutalized, she leaves Lovelace behind, and welcomes death. Her heart, she tells Anna, is "torn in pieces" (VII, 43). (Lovelace himself, confronting her death, will later acknowledge this same "incurable fracture in her heart" [VII, 348].) The heart, "more than half broken," is also, however, the heart that can no longer "dictate." At the moment of rape, Clarissa's fundamental relation to "Nature," to signs, to the "discourse of the heart" itself, changes. Her violation works as a negative revelation; it impels her toward an extended and drastic repudiation of the "science of reading men." She will no longer participate in what William Warner has called the "struggles of interpretation"; she will no longer be a reader. This choice turns out to be a repudiation of life itself.

One of Todorov's remarks on narrative again has relevance to Clarissa's history. "Death," he remarks, writing of Constant's *Adolphe*, "is nothing but the impossibility of speaking."[5] The heroine's monumentally slow and complicated exit from life—Richardson's model of pious, dignified death—is also a progressive movement away from systems of linguistic exchange. When Clarissa ceases to engage in the communicative process, the effort that has proved so disastrous to her, she also ceases to be. For the real reader, witnessing her extreme, attenuated demise, it is as if the heroine's naiveté were replaced by awareness—by melancholic recognition, finally, of deceit. Lovelace's artful demonstration of the "heartlessness" of things succeeds to this extent: with his final usage, Clarissa becomes conscious of the instability of signifying codes, and her own folly in seeking out transcendent meaning in the texts of this world, where the only available meanings are human, temporary, artificial. Rather than remain caught up in the

5. Tzvetan Todorov, *The Poetics of Prose*, trans. Richard Howard (Ithaca: Cornell University Press, 1977), p. 116.

world of "Art," which has already afflicted her beyond forebearance, where human communion turns out to be a matter of violence, and most important, perhaps, where the self (at least the female self) is given no chance of a life free of intimidation, Clarissa chooses at last the attitude of refusal. By exempting herself from discourse she exempts herself from abuse. She flies hence from the fictional world to the "next."

Clarissa's escape from interpretation extends, of course, over four volumes of Richardson's text. The process of estrangement is ghastly in one sense, in that it coincides, on the physical level, with the heroine's joyfully elongated and macabre wasting away. In another sense, however, it represents the only kind of liberation available to her. Each stage of her intricate release reflects back upon what she has gone through. Each stage confirms our sense of the inevitability—given a world without "Nature," without hermeneutic constraint—of her deathly translation.

Escape begins in an initial paroxysm—Clarissa's remarkable, savage "mad papers," her first production after the attack on her person. A deranged sequence of letters written in a "Fit" to herself and to members of her family, and which Lovelace finds, torn in pieces, on the floor of her room at Mrs. Sinclair's—these are not really communications at all, but rather, powerful images of hermeneutic fragmentation. They are the salvos of dementia and despair, but also comment, paradoxically and primitively, on Clarissa's new suspicion of the signifying medium of the letter itself. Like perverse icons, the discarded papers (made available to us in a transcription of Lovelace's) stand for a linguistic crisis. They are models of syntactic and semantic interruption; they suggest Clarissa's sense of failure, both as exegete and "scribbler."

First, the fact that the letters are written but not sent marks a basic disruption in the epistolary world, the world in which Clarissa until now has been totally absorbed. Clarissa's breaking of the epistolary circuit, represented by her failure to transmit the letter, prefigures that irrevocable stoppage of her correspondence that marks her death and the death of the fiction. Beyond this basic subversion, however, Clarissa has "torn in half" or "scratch'd thro'" the pieces of paper themselves. She has wreaked a kind of physical violence on the material artifact. When the papers are temporarily reconstituted painstakingly (and ironically) by Lovelace, the motif of fragmentation is carried over, with a kind of pathological intensity, to the semantic realm. As Richardson's editorial note reads, the contents of the letters are "affectingly incoherent." Each paper bears a message about the failure of messages, about interception, ellipsis, and the breakup of the meaningful. Thus to Anna Howe, Clarissa writes, or tries to write, of her "usage":

> O what dreadful, dreadful things have I to tell you! But yet I cannot tell you neither. . . .
> I sat down to say a great deal—My heart was full—I did not know what to say first—And thought, and grief, and confusion, and (O my poor head!) I cannot tell what—And thought, and grief, and confusion, came crouding so thick upon me: *one* would be first, *another* would be first, *all* would be first; so I can write nothing at all. [v, 327]

The mutilation of sense and syntax is linked to a loss of selfhood. In one letter, scribbled over, to Mr. Harlowe, Clarissa suspends syntactic closure, and effaces herself: "My Name is—I don't know what my name is!" (v, 328). Similarly, another letter, itself appallingly ripped up, contains a mysterious parable about a "lady" (Clarissa herself?) who is "torn in pieces" by a bear. The tale makes no sense except as self-destructive fantasy. In the case of the notorious tenth paper, finally, reconstitution of the material fragment is bootless: the paper models the disruption of orthography itself. Clarissa abolishes regular penmanship here: the page is covered with disorderly fragments of discourse; lines of writing are skewed, and run off in every direction across the page. In standard editions of *Clarissa*, the effect is created typographically (see Figure 2). Thus, as Ronald Paulson has written, citing Preston, "the printed page itself becomes a form of mimesis," a "symbolic visual object" standing in for the original written artifact that is not available.[6] The effect for the reader, however, is peculiar; and, as we shall see again shortly, it raises suspicions about the epistemological status of the text of *Clarissa* itself. None of the mad papers has a signature; they are all thus without official origin, cut off from "authority."

The violence that Clarissa, in her madness, wreaks against her writing—tearing, gapping, halving—recapitulates a phantasmic imagery of sexual violence. In light of the rape, her behavior has the quality of hysterical repetition: it seems self-destructive, a curious turning back of violence upon the self, symbolically constituted in writing. But it also points to a subliminal recognition having to do with the letter itself, and the nature of reading and writing. Clarissa's mutilation of her own discourse suggests not only an impulse toward self-destruction, but also a massive, indeed traumatic loss of faith in articulation, and the power of the letter to render meaning. What Lovelace calls her "eloquent nonsense" is the first outward sign of her changed relation to the very project of signification. The mad papers bespeak an initial despair, and an overriding sense of the failure of language—a failure equivalent, in Clarissa's terms, of course, to a failure of coherence in "Nature" itself.

Paradoxically, at the very moment Clarissa begins her arduous process of disaffiliation—following on her recovery from the mad "Fit"—she appears to those around her as a more powerful speaker and writer than ever. After her violation, her rhetoric takes on a curious, abrupt magnificence—the elo-

6. Ronald Paulson, *Emblem and Expression: Meaning in English Art in the Eighteenth Century* (Cambridge, Mass.: Harvard University Press, 1975), p. 51.

PAPER X.

LEAD me, where my own thoughts themselves may lose me;
Where I may doze out what I've left of Life,
Forget myself, and that day's guilt!—
Cruel Remembrance!—how shall I appease thee?

—Oh! you have done an act
That blots the face and blush of modesty;
Takes off the rose
From the fair forehead of an innocent Love,
And makes a blister there!—

Then down I laid my head,
Down on cold earth, and for a while was dead;
And my freed Soul to a strange Somewhere fled!
Ah! sottish Soul! said I,
When back to its cage again I saw it fly;
Fool! to resume her broken chain,
And row the galley here again!
Fool! to that Body to return,
Where it condemn'd and destin'd is to *mourn!*

O my Miss Howe! if thou hast friendship, help me,
And speak the words of peace to my divided Soul,
That wars within me,
And raises ev'ry sense to my confusion.
I'm tott'ring on the brink
Of peace; and thou art all the hold I've left!
Assist me—in the pangs of my affliction!

When Honour's lost, 'tis a relief to die:
Death's but a sure retreat from infamy.

Then farewel, Youth,
And all the joys that dwell
With Youth and Life!
And Life itself, farewel!

For Life can never be sincerely blest.
Heav'n punishes the *Bad*, and proves the *Best.*

Death only can be dreadful to the Bad
To Innocence 'tis like a bugbear dress'd
To frighten children. Pull but off the mask
And he'll appear a friend.

I could a Tale unfold—
Would harrow up thy soul!—

By swift misfortunes
How am I pursu'd!
Which on each other
Are, like waves, renew'd!

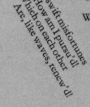

FIGURE 2. Clarissa's Tenth Mad Paper. From the Shakespeare
Head Press edition of *Clarissa* (Oxford: Basil Blackwell, 1943).

quence of outrage. Lovelace feels it. Indeed, he suffers a real (not feigned) speechlessness when he is with her, an ironic reversal of earlier situations. In the great scene in which Clarissa, lucid, storms in upon him and the "women below" while they are plotting new humiliations for her, she achieves a kind of ecstatic testimony. When she berates them for corruption, they are cowed, overwhelmed at last by her own now articulated "construction" of the events in which they all had a part. Repeatedly during this scene, Clarissa breaks in on Lovelace, frustrating his attempts to speak. "My voice was utterly broken;" he writes to Belford, "nor knew I what I said, or whether to the purpose or not" (VI, 70).

The scene shows the beginning of Lovelace's own weakening—a theme, as Elizabeth Napier has suggested, in the latter volumes of *Clarissa*.[7] Lovelace's movement toward death is a feckless, demonic parallel to Clarissa's own. His disintegration is a gradual and meandering business— culminating likewise in a death that seems at least partially or unconsciously self-willed, in the fatal duel with Colonel Morden. Lovelace is significantly unlike his victim, however, in that during his last weeks, and despite his general emotional collapse, he experiences no corresponding loss of faith in his exegetical powers. Right up to the end he is still reading (and quoting) his favored misogynistic authors, while sanctimoniously disclaiming responsibility for that "mean opinion of the [female] Sex which I had imbibed from early manhood" (VIII, 264). Regarding Clarissa, his final conclusion is that her virtuous behavior does not in fact disprove his theory of "Woman's" nature, but merely demonstrates her own unearthly, aberrant status: "As I have said and written an hundred times, there cannot be such another woman" (VIII, 264). Lovelace does not finally impugn his own fantasy construct; rather, like a medieval astronomer embellishing the Ptolemaic model of

7. Napier, p. 218.

the universe to account for comets, he simply elaborates the fiction, adding new appendages, new "maxims."

The irony of Clarissa's rhetorical strength, of course, is that it seems to come at least in part from her newfound consciousness of a basic problem, a potential fraudulence, in words themselves. When she requests her freedom from Mrs. Sinclair's house, she is sarcastic about those perversions of language she has been subjected to: "And let me hope, that I may be . . . permitted to leave this *innocent* house, as one called it (but long have my ears been accustomed to such inversions of words) as soon as the day breaks" (VI, 70). The assertion she flings at the women about their master—"Basely as he has used me, I am not his wife. He has no authority over me" (VI, 71)—again suggests radicalized perceptions, and a new contempt for the web of linguistic "constructions" in which she has been suspended.

Once Clarissa flees Lovelace and settles in at Mrs. Smith's—a place where she hopes she can live "uninterrupted for the short remainder of her life" (VI, 308)—she is apprised by Anna of more and more of his iniquities. The "wilful falshoods, repeated forgeries, and numberless perjuries" are exposed (VI, 138). Her violent antipathy to Lovelace and his associates is the result of enlightenment. But at the same time a kind of hermeneutic malaise, an unwillingness to delve further into the deceitful texts of this world, begins to overtake her. She initiates an active process of divestiture; she methodically cuts herself off from "bad Signs"—all the signifying systems that have at once fascinated and absorbed her, and contributed to her betrayal.

Clarissa's curious acts of physical self-abnegation, begun soon after her arrival at Smith's—in particular, the random distribution of her clothes and quasi-anorexic refusal to eat—seem linked, at least indirectly, to the drama of interpretation. By casting off her garments, for instance (she has Mrs. Smith give away or sell them, keeping only the plain white dress she dies in), Clarissa would seem to remove herself from the realm of sartorial meanings. As we have seen, she has been everywhere misled by sartorial signs: fashion has revealed itself as a faulty index, a denatured code. Similarly, her own dress has been deciphered by Lovelace in light of his misogynistic fictions. Clarissa's "cuffs and robings," which she has herself "curiously embroidered," have suggested to him that she must be another "ever-charming Arachne" (III, 28)—that is, beautiful and damned, a paradigm of "Woman's" pride and monstrosity. With a kind of sublime self-possession, then, she denies her own part in the system. The single white garment she retains—with its suggestion of blankness, absence, opacity—reflects an effort at self-exemption. She makes herself unavailable to interpretation according to dress—that very process which has provided her with so many deceptive pieces of information.[8] Significantly, Clarissa relates the process of denuding to death itself: as Belford tells Lovelace, she talks of dying "as if it were an occurrence as familiar to her as dressing and undressing" (VII, 276), and longs to be rid of "these *rags of mortality*" (VII, 410).

Similarly, that behavior which most appalls Mrs. Smith and Belford—Clarissa's unwillingness to consume anything besides water and a few minuscule bits of bread—suggests a repudiation of the world of signs and interpretation, with the negative emphasis shifted to her own hermeneutic activity. By refusing to ingest, to take in substances from without, she refuses to repeat that physical act which, in the case of Sinclair's tea, has led to violation. (On the phantasmic level, eating is identified, of course, with sexual penetration itself,

8. It is dubious, of course, how successful this effort at self-neutralization is, for to clothe oneself at all is always to clothe oneself in potential significance. Rather than being a kind of blank or meaning-less garment, Clarissa's plain white dress remains an *invitation* to interpreters. Those commentators who suggest its resemblance to either bridal-gown or shroud (or both) inscribe a meaning for it—that is, "write it over" with thematic significance.

and thus is perhaps even more deeply abhorrent to the heroine.) But in so doing, she would also seem to remove herself again from the necessity of interpreting phenomena. Having already misread, dreadfully, the signs of edibility, she now refrains from having to make any semantic decisions at all about the substances that are offered to her. The basic and fascinating hermeneutic problem facing all living creatures (does x bear the marks of "food" or not?) ceases to captivate her. Clarissa is unwilling to make any more determinations on the subject. Betrayed once by the instability and variability associated with the very concept of food, she saves herself, in this grotesque and perversely self-denying manner, from the task of deciphering. Paradoxically, she would rather starve herself, it now seems, than trust her own readings. Those substances looking, smelling, and tasting like food have poisoned her; no food is better than nonfood.

Clarissa's greatest act of rejection falls into place next to these preliminary gestures of denial. The most complicated abdication, of course, is from language itself—that system of signs in which, of all those codes operating in her world, she has been most deeply entangled. We have already noted the heroine's newfound suspicion of words, apparent right after the rape. In the final volumes of Richardson's novel (i.e., the final stages of her existence), Clarissa's suspicions turn into full-fledged awareness of the "heart-breaking" problem of language—the lack of constraints on utterance, the autonymous, denatured status of human discourse.

Ironically, Clarissa is writing much during her last days—letters, her will, scriptural meditations. To observers, the feverish composition looks like part of a larger praxis of self-absorption. Obsessive articulation is a form of that uncanny deathbed activity which she engages in—to the bafflement of those who are with her. Belford marvels at the bizarre "celerity" with which she writes, as well as the fact that she uses her coffin, installed in the bedroom, as a desk for "writing and reading on." What becomes apparent, however, is that Clarissa is involved in a paradoxical kind of documentation: she is everywhere using language to comment on the breakdown of language. With her final flurry of "correspondencies," she inscribes her own epiphany: "Nature" and the text are strangers to each other; read as you will.

Unlike those she has written before (or tried to write), Clarissa's letters, those to her family and Anna for instance, now seem purposely self-defeating and ambiguous structures. (The daring "Father's House" letter to Lovelace is also a paradigm of ambiguity, but because its importance is somewhat different from that of the family letters, I shall treat it separately.) Clarissa's final messages, particularly the "posthumous" letters received by the Harlowes after her death, do not include what one might expect: a last attempt to defend herself, to explain her past actions, to tell her own version of her "Story." Rather, the great theme occupying her now is the impossibility of "Story"-telling.

In a late letter to Anna, therefore, written after Anna has suggested that Clarissa write the history of her sufferings, Clarissa stresses the difficulty of such a composition when the facts of her case are themselves mysterious and elude description: "I know not by what means several of [Lovelace's] machinations to ruin me were brought about; so that some material points of my sad Story must be defective, if I were to sit down to write it" (VII, 47). She is likely, she admits, to break off unfinished any account because writing is now "so painful a task" that "could I avoid it, I would go no farther in it." (Clarissa's shocking repetition of Lovelace's leitmotiv phrase raises perplexing questions, of course, about the intentions of the "author" behind the fiction. What are we to make of this apparently gratuitous, weighty, and utterly implausible epistolary coincidence?) Clarissa seems to doubt her ability to give an authoritative reading of her own case. She foregoes, therefore, the opportunity to articulate; she voluntarily interrupts the discourse of the self.

Clarissa's unwillingness to vindicate herself here by writing an account of her usage is linked—in the public sphere—to her rejection of Cousin Morden's suggestion that she testify against Lovelace in a court of law. She now mistrusts any form of linguistic self-presentation. Her lack of faith in the power of judicial testimony is justified. Throughout *Clarissa*, legal metaphors play into the larger thematics of reading and articulation (cf. Lovelace's "perjuries"). Significantly, however, the discourse of the law is no more privileged than any other kind of discourse in the fictional world. Lovelace calls attention to this fact by his frequent allusions to the "whitening" of "black causes," and the "double-tongu'd" abilities of lawyers. As he tells Belford: "It is but glossing over one part of a Story, and omitting another, that will make a bad cause a good one at any time. What an admirable Lawyer I should have made! (VII, 74). A legal brief is as much an arbitrary "construction" as anything else; the "facts" of a situation can be interpreted and presented any way one wants. Fearing such contamination of her "Story," Clarissa thus refuses to litigate.

But a similar sense of futility informs Clarissa's letters to her relatives (VIII, letters 8–12). These letters (which we, like the Harlowes, read after she has died) together make up an odd kind of nonstatement: they do not tell the "Story" of her experience, but only allude to a narrative that *might* be written in another time and place and (now obviously) by another hand. Clarissa herself cannot write it. To James she begins, "When you come to know all my Story"—thus deferring the account itself, and since this is her last letter to him, making her own record of events eternally unavailable. Likewise, her letters to her mother and sister contain reminiscences of the "misconstructions" they have made of her behavior in the past, and suggest she is not willing to open herself further to perverse

interpretations by saying more. Her actions, she acknowledges, have had "a very ugly appearance in your eyes," but
significantly, she makes no effort now to revise their opinions
of her. All she can say to Bella, for instance, is that "No
misconstruction of her conduct" can "cancel" her sisterly
affection—a remark the only purpose of which seems to be to
remind Arabella (and us) of the hermeneutic violence that has
characterized the sister's behavior. To her Aunt Hervey,
Clarissa reiterates that her history may come to be known in
the "future," and makes the observation (now almost unbear-
ably ironic) that "uninterrupted happiness is not to be expected
in this life" (VIII, 33). In all of these utterances, there is an
anomie associated with the process of making meaning
itself—an ennui, a disinclination to reproduce experience in
language. Clarissa will no longer risk the kinds of exegetic
deformation she has suffered from the Harlowes. (Once again,
even so near the end, her fears are more than justified. The
letters describing Clarissa's situation and condition at Mrs.
Smith's which are sent to the Harlowes by their spy, the
pedant Brand, are marvels of arbitrary "construction." Relying upon incriminating misinformation gathered from the
neighbors across the street, Brand's letters model, devastat-
ingly, the autonymy of the linguistic utterance in *Clarissa*.
Jargonized to the point of inanity, they symbolize the demonic
"buzz" of language which takes the place of actual communication in the world of the novel.) Clarissa's final letters, therefore, tend toward the self-referential, the recursive. They are
opaque rather than transparent artifacts. Her words paradoxically subvert the very project of locating the truth in words;
their only message is that the narrative is always "defective,"
that the "Story" cannot be told.

Other final documents from Clarissa's pen, her scriptural
meditations and her will, are equally problematic. The fact
that she writes out extracts from the Bible in her last days
might seem at first to suggest that she has not yet given up the

search for a pure form of discourse—one that conveys meaning to the reader "naturally" and absolutely. When she reinscribes the scriptural passages, one could claim, perhaps, that Clarissa seeks here—in the text sanctioned by divine "authority"—a kind of utterance free of that instability which afflicts human texts. It is not clear, however, that this hope motivates Clarissa's acts of transcription. Rather, her apparently pious copy work conceals, again, curiously negative insinuations about language in general. Like her letters to the Harlowes, the scriptural passages Clarissa chooses have a metacritical function. More often than not, they comment, hermetically, on her own linguistic exploitation, and the essential uselessness of words, except as tools of violence. One such meditation, addressed to the Harlowes, begins: "How long will ye vex my soul, and break me in pieces with words!" (VII, 136). Again: "Why will ye write bitter words against me, and make me possess the iniquities of my youth?" Language avails itself everywhere as an instrument of aggression. "If your soul were in my soul's stead, I also could speak as you do: I could heap up words against you." Similarly, in the meditation transparently inspired by Lovelace and entitled by Clarissa "On being hunted after by the Enemy of my Soul," the "evil man" is one with a sharpened (i.e., "penetrating") tongue:

> *Deliver me, O Lord, from the evil man. Preserve me from the violent man.*
> Who *imagines mischief in his heart.*
> He *hath sharpened* his *tongue like a serpent. Adder's poison is under* his *lips.* [VII, 164]

The indictment is consistent; discourse everywhere threatens injury to the innocent. It is a weapon of evil.

One must add as an aside that, given the unconstrained cutting and excerpting of documents going on elsewhere in

Clarissa, Clarissa's own activity of selective extraction, which unwittingly violates the integrity of the scriptural text, is a troubling one. Editorial violence—typically represented by those excisions, erasures, and rearrangements performed by Lovelace on Clarissa's and Anna's correspondence—has been a literal counterpart always to the hermeneutic violence readers wage against authorial intentions. We may wonder, indeed, how much Clarissa's own act of textual interference consciously or unconsciously recapitulates the general syndrome associated with reading in the fiction. In one light, her extracts hint at the vulnerability of *all* texts—Scripture included—to the manipulations of the reader.

Belford, interestingly enough, is impressed by Clarissa's piety, and tries to imitate her by beginning his own program of Scripture reading. Lovelace's scorn when he hears this news reminds us of his earlier dismissal of the Bible as "a fine piece of ancient history." His blasphemy has been a theme throughout the novel: for him, Scripture is but another piece of literature, another great text available for mishandling and irresponsible citation. As a number of commentators point out, Lovelace's frivolities on the subject of Holy Writ suggest, of course, his exemption from the Christian state of grace. But the real reader is subtly implicated in this flippancy. Again, what *is* the epistemological status of Scripture, given the compromised vision of the text operating in *Clarissa?* Lovelace's equation of Scripture and poetry invites us to consider, at least for a moment, the same equation, thereby obscuring any theological point. His impieties work subversively, suggesting again the possibility that no text can claim transcendent authority, that all texts are equally fictional constructs, created by human imagination alone. Nothing else in *Clarissa,* as we have seen, works hard to erase this possibility.

Like the meditations, Clarissa's will bespeaks her new awareness of the polysemousness of words. One might say that the will registers her knowledge officially: it is a formal gesture, yet as paradoxical as any other. The text of the will shows Clarissa fully conscious of the conflicting interpretations readers will make of the testament itself. Much of this highly self-conscious document, therefore, is devoted to anticipating the variability that will afflict its own reading. Clarissa's melancholy preamble implicitly acknowledges the danger in interpretation—"cavils about words." "I have heard," she writes, "of so many instances of confusion and disagreement in families; and so much doubt and difficulty, for want of absolute clearness in the Testaments of departed persons" (VIII, 105). However, apart from deciding to compose her will while still physically and psychologically strong enough to do so, Clarissa ceases to strive for "absolute clearness." Her response to the threat of conflicting interpretations is at once illuminating and disarming: she invents and incorporates in the text itself a curiously flawed statistical method for her readers to use in deciding the meaning of the will. In case of disputes resulting from "omissions and imperfections" in the document, Cousin Morden, Belford, and Anna are to compare their individual readings, and "provided [one "construction"] be unanimous . . . direct it to be put into force, as if I had so written and determined myself" (VIII, 124). A perception of the insufficiency of the written artifact is present, almost palpably, in these instructions. On one level, the implication is that the will alone does not make itself clear: three unusually privileged readers are needed to fill out its gaps, to produce a satisfactory meaning for it. Beyond this, however, the unanimity clause raises, without resolving, the possibility that even these most sympathetic readers—the three persons most attuned to Clarissa's desires—may disagree about meaning. What is to be done if this happens is not made clear. One could say that Clarissa's proposal for obviating textual indeterminacy is itself a crux, and thus defeats, pathetically, its own purpose. Still, peculiarities aside, Clarissa's instructions to her readers institutionalize the crucial perception: interpretations are creative, arbitrary—imposed from without on the imperfect object. The concluding pathos in all of these prepa- rations, of course, is that they really do nothing at all to stop the endless cycle of misreadings. After the reading of the will at Harlowe-Place, Morden writes to Belford that the Har- lowes "shewed themselves to be true Will-disputants" (VIII, 126). In her own home, dead Clarissa is still being construed, wantonly and unfavorably, at the last. "Some other passages in the Will were called *flights, and such whimsies as distinguish people of imagination from those of judgment*" (VIII, 127).

Before her death, it must be allowed, Clarissa has one lim- ited rhetorical triumph—the celebrated "Father's House" communiqué sent to Lovelace (VII, Letter 52). The triumph is an equivocal and disturbing one for the reader, in that the only function of this letter is to ensure that Clarissa will be able to die "uninterrupted," but the textual stratagem she deploys here suggests again the radicalization of her relationship to language. This marvelous distressed piece of wit is Clarissa's own ironically Lovelacean exploitation of semantic variability. By writing "I am setting out with all diligence for my Father's House" (VII, 189), Clarissa intends, as she claims in her expla- nation to Anna, to describe her imminent death and transfig- uration. At the same time, however, she knows full well that Lovelace will read the crucial passage literally, and think she means she is going back to Harlowe-Place. (The device indeed effectively keeps him from seeking her out at Smith's.) The letter is a paradigm of indeterminacy—turned back on her oppressor. She anticipates for once *his* interpretation, and is able to manipulate him in precisely the way he has formerly manipulated her—by exploiting the gap between the linguistic sign and "Nature," between words and objects or events in the world. Ambiguity is the distinguishing feature of the dena- tured utterance.

The fact that the heroine (as well as Richardson the "Editor") refers to her letter as "Allegorical" is thus overwhelmingly suggestive, in light of the larger thematics of reading. Clarissa is fully aware, in some technical sense, that her coup depends upon polysemousness, the dissolve of single, fixed meanings. She presents Lovelace with an open-ended text, knowing (because she knows his desire) how he will shape its meaning. Allegory has always been recognized as that literary form which calls attention most starkly to the ultimately nonreferential (and hence indeterminate) nature of linguistic structures. Unlike its traditional counterpart—symbolism—allegory dramatizes the split between word and world, and makes us uniquely conscious of our own interpretative freedom. In classic symbolic texts, Jonathan Culler writes, "the process of interpretation is made to seem natural," so that we seem to experience "a fusion of the concrete and the abstract, of the appearance and the reality of form and meaning." The symbol, it is supposed, is "a natural sign in which *signifiant* and *signifié* are indissolubly fused, not an arbitrary or conventional sign in which they are linked by human authority or habit." Allegory, by contrast, "stresses the difference between levels, flaunts the gap we must leap to produce meaning, and thus displays the activity of interpretation in all its conventionality." It "recognizes the impossibility of fusing the empirical and the eternal and thus demystifies the symbolic relation."[9] In Paul de Man's phrase, allegory depends on a "semantic dissonance"—the noncoincidence of proper and literal meanings of the allegorical figure.[10]

Clarissa's own "allegorical" gesture attests to such a dissociation between language and reference. It allows for the work of the reader in supplying meaning. She is not without qualms, of course, about making use of so "extraordinary" a ploy. Psychologically speaking, it is clear she cannot trans-

9. Jonathan Culler, *Structuralist Poetics* (Ithaca: Cornell University Press, 1975), pp. 229–30.
10. Paul de Man, *Allegories of Reading: Figural Language in Rousseau, Nietzsche, Rilke, and Proust* (New Haven: Yale University Press, 1979), p. 74.

form her momentary strategy of control into a continuous practice. A certain melancholia informs her decision to exploit Lovelace's reading: her act is born out of disillusionment alone, and is not a sign of willingness to participate further (or more effectively) in the human hermeneutic struggle. She is afraid, as the summary of one of her letters to Anna notes, that the tricky letter "is a step that is not strictly right, if Allegory or Metaphor be not allowable to one in her circumstances" (VII, 253). The discourse of the "heart" fails; yet Clarissa is profoundly uneasy with the only available substitute—this Lovelacean discourse of the "head." Her "strange step" leaves her feeling guilty and disordered. Thus, in the same letter in which she describes her ploy to Anna Howe, the "heart" takes its sudden, ominous, implacable revenge. "—But I am very ill—I must drop my Pen—A sudden Faintness overspreads my heart—Excuse my crooked writing!—Adieu, my dear!—Adieu!" (VII, 254). The disintegration of utterance here foreshadows her now imminent passage out of the realm of "crooked writing"—the denatured linguistic code—altogether. "I never was so very oddly affected," she appends to the letter a moment later. "Something that seemed totally to overwhelm my faculties—I don't know how to describe it—I believe I do amiss in writing so much."

7

The Death of the Author: Clarissa's Coffin

In death, escape is final. Given the distended internal drama of interpretation—the welter of readings and misreadings, of meanings formed and suspended and deformed—Clarissa's death scene has its alternately poignant and black-humorish resonances. Death confirms (pathetically? ironically?) Clarissa's loss of utterance; it is the ultimate form of interruption. Throughout Belford's description of the scene, the heroine's growing speechlessness is the primary index to the process of dissolution. At the start she is "moving her lips without uttering a word." The vocal hesitations increase in frequency: she speaks haltingly to Belford and the rest in a "faint inward voice," with "broken periods" and "broken accents" (VIII, 2–3). Belford's account is in fact redundant to the point of obsession: he returns again and again to this loss of the voice, and the breaking of speech. Unlike more conventional deathbed narrative—including Belford's own report on Mrs. Sinclair's bestial demise, where he uses a variety of physical symptoms to signal approaching death—there is little elegant variation here. The effect of Belford's rhetoric is paradigmatic rather than naturalistic: dying, Clarissa is refined to a (failing) vocal presence, a fitting reminder of her basic doomed search, throughout the fiction, for discourse itself. By the end Clarissa struggles to say anything at all. Belford's letter mimics the struggle typographically, puncturing the written record of her last words with dashes—a basic visual sign of division and interruption.

> She waved her hand to us both, and bowed her head six several times, as we have since recollected, as if distinguishing every person present... and she spoke falteringly and inwardly,—Bless—bless—bless—you All—And now—And now—[holding up her almost lifeless hands for the last time] Come—O come—Blessed Lord—JESUS! [VIII, 5]

The consummate twist here, of course, is that Belford's transcription itself produces a kind of closure which does not exist in actuality: the last of Clarissa's words, we are told, the name of her savior, remains half-spoken. As she expires, her crucial invocation is cut off midway, and lingers in the air "but half-pronounced." Clarissa dies then, as she has lived—with the "Story" unfinished, and meaning amended by the ever helpful "reader," an aftereffect.

Clarissa does not die, however, without leaving a memento, the last, and perhaps most important text within *Clarissa*, a posthumous token for her many readers. I have deferred speaking of the heroine's coffin—that strange emblem of her morbidity—even though it plays a part in the fiction before her actual death. Readers of Richardson's novel have always felt the image of the coffin to have a powerful closural force, as well as an encompassing symbolic relation to other elements in Clarissa's history. Alan Wendt describes the coffin as the "central symbol" in the fiction, one that merges the "great themes" of sex and death.[1] Yet this summarizing force must be recast, it seems to me, in light of the theme we have so far followed out: the problem of interpretation. Ingeniously in-

---

1. Alan Wendt, "Clarissa's Coffin," *Philological Quarterly*, 34 (1960), 481–82.

scribed by Clarissa herself, the coffin is an irresistible hermeneutic object. Its relevance to its "author," the dying heroine, seems uncanny, its devices intricate and mysterious. It demands explanation; it demands "penetration." It is, in short, quite insanely appealing. Most important, the coffin fixes attention on two levels at once: it presents itself to the gaze of readers within the fiction, yet it also holds a promise of meaning out to the real reader. What do we make of it? Our curiosity coincides with that of the fictional characters, the heroine's survivors.

This double hermeneutic investment that Clarissa's last "House" elicits—at once from us and from our counterparts within the fiction—serves to remind us, however, of that general structural phenomenon noted at the outset: the simultaneity, given the epistolary format, of two interpretative acts, the fictional reader's and the real reader's. At all points in *Clarissa*, as I suggested earlier, our reading mirrors the inner process. When we attempt to interpret the epistolary text, when we look for its "Story," we repeat the activity of characters attempting to decipher experience, reified, paradigmatically, in those smaller texts, the letters, which make up the larger text we read. I proposed at the start the usefulness of moving from the inner reading history to the outer one, and to this end have looked in some detail at the thematicization of interpretation within the novel. The interest of Clarissa's coffin first of all is that it finishes off, in some sense, this primary history; it is a final text to be interpreted by fictional readers—particularly significant because it subsumes (actually, consumes) that which until now has been the central hermeneutic subject in the fictional world—the subject of violence—Clarissa's own body. Yet precisely because it is a last text of a sort, it directs us in compelling wise, once again, to the issue of our own reading, and what will be our final concern here—the reader's relation to the text of *Clarissa* itself. Clarissa's "House," one could say, is also a bridge—for her, from this world to the "next," for us, from a realm of fictional readers to a realm of real ones.

Before the heroine's death, her coffin is already associated, on two counts, with textuality. To the dismay of her friends at Mrs. Smith's, Clarissa uses the coffin, installed in her bed-chamber, as household fixture—as a "desk" on which she "writes and reads" (VII, 359). But she writes "on" it, of course, in two senses: the lid itself is a kind of articulation, inscribed with the various scriptural texts and emblematic devices she has chosen for it—the broken lily, "an Hour-glass Winged," an urn, and "a crowned Serpent, with its tail in its mouth, forming a ring" (VII, 338). Clarissa's name and deathdate (pro-jected) appear inside the annulus. The coffin, thus, is a mes-sage, or, at least, a simulation of one. It is a sentence of sorts, employing a peculiarly mixed, almost rebus-like syntax—juxtaposing verbal information (the scriptural fragments and proper name) against an odd visual iconography, half-conventional (serpent-emblem and the hourglass), half Claris-sa's private estranging vision (the broken stem of the lily).

Yet the important point to be made about this final *writing* is precisely that its point is unclear. It is at once fascinating and utterly opaque, its meaning indeterminate. Significantly, Clarissa dies without providing any extraneous commentary, any gloss, on her mysterious coffin-text. In the profoundest sense, it is her "last word." She is mute thereafter, unavailable for comment. The question of meaning is transferred, definitively—to the reader.

Within the fictional world, the coffin indeed inspires a ver-itable orgy of reading. We witness this glut of reading anec-doctally, through the narrative of Colonel Morden, who brings Clarissa's corpse to Harlowe-Place. His letter to Bel-ford on this occasion contains vignettes of interpretation—descriptions, almost tableaux, showing Clarissa's relatives and acquaintances as they view the coffin and attempt to "pene-trate" its meaning. Everyone is revealed in the moment of exegesis—caught in the act of deciphering. On the approach to the Harlowes', for instance, the villagers are the first to be enthralled by the sight of the coffin, and immediately "re-mark" in wonder at the emblems, "the more, when they were told, that all were of [Clarissa's] own ordering" (VIII, 77). "The plates, and emblems, and inscriptions set everyone gazing upon it" (VIII, 77). When the funeral party arrives at Harlowe-Place, all, Morden writes, are "led on by an impulse they could not resist" toward the gloomy spectacle. The Har-lowes react variously to Clarissa's last text. Clarissa's mother's response is instantaneous and histrionic: "The poor Lady but just cast her eye upon the coffin, and then snatched it away, retiring with passionate grief towards the window" (VIII, 78). Mr. Harlowe is described "fetching a heavy groan" at the sight of the emblems. Arabella and the uncles return compulsively to the insignias, unable to look away for long: "The Uncles and the Sister looked and turned away, looked and turned away, very often upon the emblems, in silent sorrow" (VIII, 79). Aunt Hervey makes curious literal contact with the texts and designs on the coffin—reinscribing them, surreally, with her own tears, until they are obscured. "[She] could read no farther," Morden tells Belford; "her tears fell in large drops upon the plate she was contemplating" (VIII, 79). James Har-lowe, in contrast, seems more or less hypnotized by what he sees on the coffin lid, and studies it with "fixed attention." Ironically, Morden's description of James in the act of reading is itself contaminated by the prevailing motif of the text. When James looks on Clarissa's funeral devices, his features seem to Morden "imprinted" with feeling, and his very countenance a kind of embossed surface, waiting to be read—almost a parody of the coffin itself. Morden obliges then, gratuitously, with his own interpretation of James's face. "Yet, I dare say, [he] knew not a symbol or letter upon [the lid] at that moment, had the question been asked him. In a profound reverie he stood, his arms folded, his head on one side, and marks of stupefaction imprinted upon every feature" (VIII, 77). Finally (again at least according to Morden), Anna Howe seems unusually quick to draw significance from the coffin-text. What she discerns in her friend's dismal memorial, however, is by no means transparent. "Surveying the lid, she seemed to take in at once the meaning of the emblems" (VIII, 88). Morden does not elaborate further.

Strikingly, Morden's vignettes dramatize from without that syndrome which, as we have seen, has been continuously figured throughout *Clarissa*—the anarchism of the reader. We should not be misled by Morden's own glosses on what he sees: that is, his assumption that Anna reads the coffin-text correctly (whatever a correct reading might entail), or that James reads deviously or uncomprehendingly. The point is that everyone is reading, and their reading is apparently private, alienated, idiosyncratic. The eccentricities of facial expression and diversity of physical gesture demonstrated by the coffin's different viewers witness implicitly to the multiplicity of their unarticulated "constructions." Meaning has become, it would seem, an intensely and wholly personal matter. The coffin itself *says* nothing, but acts as a site for individual discoveries—of guilt, of compassion, of bitterness. It inspires as many interpretations as it has interpreters; readers read it according to subjective emotional states. No consensus, finally, is dramatized in Morden's detailed account, no collective enlightenment regarding any ultimate meaning. Instead, the process of interpretation is exposed as a form of solipsism, a mode of estrangement.

Considered as text, then, as work of Clarissa's dying "Art," the coffin functions in a manner antithetical to that of T. S. Eliot's famous "objective correlative." Rather than being the "formula" for one "*particular* emotion," the coffin allows for an excess of contradictory reactions—one for each new reader. There is nothing inevitable about it. Interestingly enough, we have the inescapable sensation that Clarissa herself—dead and immune at last—has somehow planned it that way. The juxtaposed texts and emblems are ostentatiously mysterious. They have a madly purposive kind of obscurity, a teasing ambiguity—almost as if Clarissa intended a game with her surviving "readers," and indeed anticipated the subjectivity of their responses.

She catches us out too, of course, with the puzzle she sets. As I suggested before, real readers are absorbed into the motley company of interpreters. Our natural wish is to make sense of Clarissa's inscription, to translate or paraphrase it, to locate a meaning for it. Yet so open-ended, so fragmented a structure is the coffin-text, that it opens itself to virtually any kind of critical recuperation. Different translations emerge, depending on one's favored mode of reading. One need only rehearse a few of these to find a paradigm for the subjectivity of *critical* readers. Clarissa's coffin can be interpreted historically, for instance, in light of eighteenth-century emblem-books, conventional iconographic systems, and memorial symbolism. Margaret Doody has commented on the connection between Clarissa's coffin devices and traditional images preserved in emblem-books of the period.[2] The "flying Hour-glasses, Death-heads, Spades, Mattocks, and Eternity" of which Belford dreams after viewing the heroine's coffin are symbols that appear in works such as George Wither's *A Collection of Emblemes, Ancient and Moderne* (1635). Similarly, as Wendt has pointed out, the coffin's combination of texts and devices can be made to carry a number of contemporary theological connotations—particularly with relevance to seventeenth- and eighteenth-century devotional literature of the kind Richardson and his audience were familiar with.

Simultaneously, however, other sorts of reading are possible. The juxtaposition of the icon of rupture and frag-

2. Margaret A. Doody, *A Natural Passion: A Study of the Novels of Samuel Richardson* (London: Oxford University Press at the Clarendon Press, 1974), p. 186, n. 1.

mentation—the broken lily—with the icon of closure—the ourobourus—allows for what one might call anthropological interpretation. The binary opposition figured by the coffin devices may remind us of those symbolic structural oppositions which Lévi-Strauss has isolated in the myths of traditional societies. We may be led in turn to a strictly formal analysis of the fiction of the whole—using the rhetorical figure of the antithesis as a guiding principle. On classically structuralist grounds, a case can be made, indeed, that antithesis is the controlling semantic function in *Clarissa*—and the basic shape of the novel's structure of meaning. The interplay of paired terms throughout the fiction—"Black" and "White," "Art" and "Nature," "Angel" and "Woman," and so on— suggests as much, of course; but plot itself is generated out of fundamental oppositions. Early on Anna writes of Clarissa's moral plight: "What a fatality, that you have no better an option—Either a *Scylla* or a *Charybdis*!" (II, 66). (One is reminded of Joyce's linking of the figure of the antithesis with the formal intricacies of the "Scylla and Charybdis" chapter in *Ulysses*.)

Finally, though by no means exhausting interpretative possibilities, one could treat Clarissa's emblems graphemically, as per certain kinds of semiotic analysis. Do we find, for example, an inverted version of an L (as in Lovelace) in the image of the broken-stemmed lily (Ꞁ)? Or a closed-off transformation of Clarissa's C in the serpent-figure (O)? Given the motif of the "Cypher" in Clarissa's history and the disarming tendency of the fiction to merge naturalistic and textual levels (Sinclair's infamous "House," with front and back wings connected by a passageway(⊐⊏), repeats the H of both "Harlowe" and "Harlot"), the location of a primitive symbolic alphabet in the coffin emblems is not, perhaps, as frivolous as it might at first seem.

Following out any of these interpretative avenues (and I have only sketched out various starting points for extended analyses), we take Clarissa up on her dare. Yet again, the crucial point is that all the hermeneutic possibilities exist simultaneously: none excludes the others, and none has finally an epistemologically privileged relation to the message it purports to decipher—the coffin itself. We can rewrite the coffin-text any way we please.

I mentioned before that in life Clarissa offers no delimitations on the meaning of her strange message. In an ironic turnabout—in which the real reader is implicated—she solicits unconstrained interpretation. Without preface, she invites "penetration." There is a self-conscious, epiphanic quality to her gesture—as if, having suffered the violence of being read by others, she now paradoxically *seeks* readers, yet on her own terms. Her personal exemption from violence will be ensured by death, of course. But with a kind of perverse jokesomeness (the hodgepodge of words and symbols on the coffin recollects Addison's examples of "false wit"), she leaves behind a mystifying substitute for the self—a new text to take the place of that other, primary text, her body itself. The joke stops only for Lovelace—the one person prohibited by the heroine from viewing the coffin, the one reader excluded from the final conglomeration of exegetes. Politically, this exclusion can be construed as a last-gasp triumph for Clarissa over her bogey; formally, it signals Lovelace's own now imminent departure from the world of reading—that is, his death. Still, this one bitter exception apart, all are invited to decipher; all are enjoined to read. Free at last from her oppressors, Clarissa indulges them—and us—with a last sublime "Whimsey," the unimpeachable wit of the dead.

If Clarissa formulates her coffin as a text, the fact remains, however, that it is also a coffin. Like a dream-object, it condenses two functions. And here one feels the full revelatory force of Clarissa's final act of inscription. The coffin is a text that encases, literally, its own dead author. To "penetrate" the engraved lid is also to confront a corpse. If we sense a paradigmatic quality in this ultimately hallucinatory spectacle—Clarissa tucked away, like a letter in an envelope, in her grotesquely "written-on" box—the reason for it, I think, is precisely this: the coffin is a literalization of that hermeneutic situation which has conditioned Clarissa's tragedy. One could say it is a concretized metaphor for textuality itself. It lacks "authority," utterly and abysmally— because the author is in fact dead: mute and eternally hidden from view, inside yet inaccessible. All that is left is the inscription itself, the surface—estranged from being, cut off from any human presence, any "natural" point of origin. The coffin-text is a residue, a sign of absence. As such, it can guarantee no ultimate meaning; its intrinsic content is "Nothing." (An aside from Clarissa, on the prolixity of her personal testament: "So much written . . . about what will be Nothing when this writing comes to be opened and read, will be excused when my present unhappy circumstances and absence from all my natural friends are considered" [VIII, 108].) With the author absent, the message one thinks to unravel remains perpetually unverifiable, indeterminate. Readings (as we have seen) multiply, and challenge one another. A politics of meaning is born. The coffin is representative, then, of all those signs—verbal and visual—which, lacking the infusion of "Nature," have led Clarissa to her catastrophe. Simultaneously it suggests the letter itself, the basic textual unit in *Clarissa*. Like the letter, its existence is motivated by occultation, the disappearance of the authorial body. We must piece out its meaning on our own.

In Roland Barthes's essay "The Death of the Author" (1968), the image that Clarissa's coffin so powerfully reifies— that of the dead author—takes its place in an explanatory critical myth, as central trope for a new poetics of reading. Barthes invokes the "death" of the author in order to figure rhetorically the collapse of authorial constraints on textual interpretation, and to promote his theory that it is the reader who actually "produces" the text. Speaking of a paradigmatic writing, Barthes suggests that it will trace "the destruction of every voice, of every point of origin." "Writing is that neutral, composite, oblique space where our subject slips away, the negative where all identity is lost, starting with the very identity of the body writing."[3] At least since the Reformation and the discovery of "the prestige of the individual," he proposes, the meaning of a given text has always been sought "in the man or woman who produced it, as if it were always in the end, through the more or less transparent allegory of the fiction, the voice of a single person, the *author* 'confiding' in us." "To give the text an Author"—to appeal to intentionality, to "authority" itself—is "to impose a limit on the text, to furnish it with a final signified, to close the writing."[4] When this phantasmic "Author" is removed from consideration, however, Barthes posits, the shape of reading is radically altered. A revolutionary hermeneutics is instituted: one no longer consumes an authorial meaning; one produces one's own.

> In the multiplicity of writing, everything is to be disentangled, nothing deciphered; the structure can be followed, "run" (like the thread of a stocking) at every point and at every level, but there is nothing beneath: the space of writing is to be ranged over, not pierced; writing ceaselessly posits meaning ceaselessly to evaporate it, carrying out a systematic exemption of meaning.[5]

The "birth of the reader," Barthes concludes, "must be at the cost of the death of the Author."

As Clarissa dies, then, a multitude of readers are born—her "Friends," her enemies, and of course the real reader, who may

3. Roland Barthes, "The Death of the Author," in *Image-Music-Text*, trans. Stephen Heath (New York: Hill & Wang, 1977), p. 142.
4. Barthes, "Death of the Author," p. 147.
5. Barthes, p. 147.

be friend or enemy. Representing a gesture of inscription rather than expression, the heroine's coffin is the concluding opacity upon which *Clarissa* suspends. It initiates a last untrammeled process of reading, the same process which has everywhere shaped Clarissa's tragic history.

8

The Death of the Author:
Richardson and the Reader

There is another dead author, of course. Samuel Richardson has left behind his own coffin-text, his own intricate fantasia and challenge to readers—the text of *Clarissa* itself. Like his heroine, he is absent from us, concealed behind the dense, ornate surface of his fiction, silenced by a continuous gabble of imaginary voices, among which that of the "Editor" who shares his name is only one more, albeit pompous addition to the cacophony. Where is Richardson? Can we "penetrate" the tangled mass of *Clarissa* itself and find him there—an immutable source of meaning, our "authority"?

The questions are setups, obviously. A novel that thematizes the denatured status of texts and the anarchy of readers, as I have suggested already, raises inevitable questions about its own status and its own readers. The internal drama of *Clarissa*, as we have seen, radicalizes our sense of how things signify. It induces what one might call semiotic catharsis. Along with the heroine, the reader is caught, not in a world where meaning flows from "Nature," but one where it is a function of "Art" alone—the art of the perceiver. Our very sense of the "natural" is disrupted, then abolished. Yet this radicalization we undergo extends inevitably to our view of

that larger, more complicated sign system that is the text itself. *Clarissa* is afflicted by the general hermeneutic instability
of the fictional world. Out of the inchoate, coy, obfuscatory
mass of the fiction—where no single voice prevails—the
reader must "construct" meaning, impose an order on events.
Clarissa activates the invention, the "penetration"—the desire
of the reader. Any "authority" one may wishfully invest in the
historical imago—Richardson—is naught, finally, in face of
this desire. For *Clarissa*, like its eponymous heroine, is rewritten by each new reader. And in the moment of reading, meaning is always a matter of "Art"—not that of a historical author,
but one's own.

The categories of "Nature" and "Art" (emerging so conve-
niently from the fiction itself) suggest a critical context in which
we may explore these premises. The terms are those associated, of course, with the ancient theory of mimesis, and
that critical tradition which holds that the artwork is a
simulacrum of external reality, "a mirror held up to Nature."
What I have said can indeed be reformulated in relation to the
mimetic theory of narrative: *Clarissa* challenges the mimetic
assumption.

The concept of mimesis, applied to narrative, originates in
what Jonathan Culler has called the basic convention govern-
ing the reading of fictional works: our expectation that the
work will reflect or represent a recognizable world.[1] The
myth underlying the concept is Platonic in structure: the
"world" (Nature) is felt to be ontologically prior to the linguistic artifact, which is only a recapitulation of that which already exists. But the myth veils, of course, a much more
complex phenomenological situation. We recuperate fictional
elements in light of our conception of "the way things are."
We seek conformities between the fictional world and our

1. Jonathan Culler, *Structuralist Poetics* (Ithaca: Cornell University
Press, 1975), p. 189.

149

own; we seek details that verify what Culler has called the "mimetic contract," that corroborate our sense of things. Yet this very sense of things, as I noted before in the discussion of cultural codes, is itself a fictional structure, an "as-if" construction, formulated by the individual in response to cultural convention. The process of reading fiction, then, is a process of naturalization: the reader attempts to organize the text in terms of an image of Nature, which is itself subjectively grounded, conventional, projective. So-called mimetic works are not those, therefore, which represent external reality, pure and simple. Rather, they are works that the reader is able to charge with meaning, in accordance with his or her own fiction of the real.

Narratives can and do suspend the mimetic contract, of course. By calling attention to the convention of referentiality itself, certain texts frustrate readers' attempts to naturalize them. In so doing, they simultaneously make us aware of the arbitrary, subjective shape of our own models of intelligibility, and the projective nature of the reading process itself. The *nouveau roman* of the 1950s and 1960s is a paradigmatic (and some might say kitschy) example of the fiction that self-consciously challenges the reader's ability to organize it according to conventional models of coherence. As Culler notes, the process of recognition is blocked in such works, thereby undermining the reader's cherished "referential illusion." "Robbe-Grillet's famous description (in *Les Gommes*) of a tomato slice, which tells us first that it is perfect and then that it is flawed, plays on the fact that this description at first appears to have a purely referential function, which is troubled when the writing introduces uncertainties and thus lifts our attention away from a supposed object to the process of writing itself."[2] We are forced to confront the text as an autonymous verbal structure, separate from any image of Nature

2. Culler, p. 193.

we may try to impose on it. By subverting the notion of referentiality, the "new novel" thus exposes the reader's own act of ordering in all its conventionality. And if our way of reading the text is exposed for what it is—as an active process of producing meaning in accordance with previously internalized models of intelligibility—so too, one must conclude, is our way of reading (i.e., interpreting and defining) the world itself.

But earlier works also make similar exposures. *Tristram Shandy* is the exemplary case in eighteenth-century literature of a self-consciously literary artifact. With its narrative pops and stuttering, bollixed time sequence, and uncontrollably wild typography, Tristram's contorted life story is in fact a nonstory, an antimimesis. Everywhere the metacritical function of the writing overtakes and consumes the representational. Readers cannot lose themselves in the illusion of referentiality: we are made as unrelievedly conscious of ourselves as readers as Tristram is of himself as a writer.

Yet so persistent is *Tristram Shandy*'s exploration of narrative conventions, and so intense its critique of the reader's mimetic assumptions, it has tended to keep us from seeing antimimetic elements in other fictional works of the period. In *The Rise of the Novel*, for instance (a book that has done much to institutionalize a certain view of the relationships between the major eighteenth-century novelists), Ian Watt sharply distinguishes Sterne's "parody of a novel" and its challenge to "the ultimate realist premise of a one-to-one correspondence between literature and reality" from the more typically and straightforwardly "realistic" fictions of Defoe, Richardson, and Fielding.[3] In the case of Richardson at least, this distinction is somewhat overstated. What Watt calls Richardson's "realism of presentation"—his method of signifying

3. Ian Watt, *The Rise of the Novel* (Berkeley: University of California Press, 1957), p. 290.

psychological experience through the use of a "more minutely discriminated time-scale, and less selective attitude to what should be told the reader"—should not distract us from the many features of his novels which subvert the premises of formal realism. Watt slights the rather more paradoxical nature of Richardson's fiction—particularly *Clarissa*, which at once feigns a world of human experience, and undermines its own feigning in various ways. Indeed, just as Clarissa is disabused of her innocent sense of the relation between human texts and her vision of "Nature," so the real reader faces an analogous illumination: *Clarissa* repeatedly strips us of our complacent faith in its own representational illusion. The result is that we are forced to revise our concept of the text itself—no longer perceiving it as the reflected image of a human reality, a simulacrum of events through which the author succeeds in conveying a certain meaning to us, but as the function of our own unconstrained constructive operations.

It is the peculiar nature of the epistolary form, as I noted at the outset, which makes us conscious of reading—and, paradigmatically, of its freedom. One can say this another way: the letter form itself is primarily responsible for the disruption of the mimetic illusion. Richardson, of course, would not have agreed. In the postscript to *Clarissa* he quotes with admiration the "ingenious and candid Foreigner" (Albrecht von Haller, whose translated remarks on the novel appeared in *Gentleman's Magazine* for June and August of 1749), who praises the epistolary method for creating a more realistic effect than other kinds of narration. "[This manner of writing] has given the author great advantages, which he could not have drawn from any other species of narration. The minute particulars of events, the sentiments and conversations of the parties, are, upon this plan, exhibited with all the warmth and spirit, that the passion supposed to be predominant at the very time, could produce, and with all the distinguishing characteristics which memory can supply in a History of recent transactions" (VIII, 326). In contrast, first- and third-person

narration, found in the "Romance," depend upon gross impro-
babilities: "They suppose the History to be written after the
series of events is closed by the catastrophe: A circumstance
which implies a strength of memory beyond all example and
probability in the persons concerned, enabling them, at the
distance of several years, to relate all the particulars of a tran-
sient conversation: Or rather, it implies a yet more improbable
confidence and familiarity between all these persons and the
author." The "Foreigner" does make one objection regarding
the credibility of the epistolary form—that it requires that "all
the characters should have an uncommon taste for this kind of
conversation, and that they should suffer no event, nor even a
remarkable conversation, to pass, without immediately com-
mitting it to writing"—but Richardson swiftly denies that this
feature raises problems in *Clarissa*. "It is presumed," he
writes, "that what this gentleman says of the difficulties attending a Story thus given in the Epistolary manner of writing, will not be found to reach the History before us" (VIII,
327). It is "very well accounted for," he continues, how the
four major correspondents—Clarissa, Anna, Lovelace, and
Belford—come to take "so great a delight" in letter writing.
Thus the illusion of verisimilitude is maintained. As for the
excessive length to which the epistolary novel must run,
owing to the exhaustive record of events and conversations, it
but increases the pleasure, Richardson concludes, that the
"Person of Taste" will receive from a "well-drawn Picture of
Nature" (VIII, 330).[4]

4. There is a suggestion that Richardson may not have been quite as
oblivious in practice to the problem here as he seems to be in the Preface.
See, for instance, his letter to Aaron Hill (20 January 1745/6), written
during the composition of *Clarissa*: "Length is my principal Disgust at present. . . . The fixing of Dates has been a Task to me. I am afraid I make the
Writers do too much in the Time." (Cited in George Sherburn's introduction to the Riverside edition of *Clarissa* [Boston: Houghton Mifflin, 1962], p.
xii.) Sherburn notes that "within the period from 6 A.M. to midnight of June
10, Lovelace along with normal activities of the day is supposed to write
something like 14,000 words" (p. xii).

The problem raised by the otherwise sympathetic "Foreigner," however, is not one that can be quite so easily dismissed. Indeed, he has hit upon the essential difficulty with the epistolary format. The novel in letters attempts a uniquely mediated kind of mimesis: it mimes Nature obliquely, by imitating a series of pseudo-historical documents that supposedly give the reader access to a world of events and persons, the world of experience. Yet paradoxically, the distinguishing feature of the epistolary text—the mediacy of the letter—is that very aspect which ultimately disrupts the reader's ability to regard it indefinitely as a "Picture of Nature." There is something wrong with the letter: it is too insistent, too much with us as we read.

Richardson is unwilling to admit anything problematic in the epistolary situation. But the awkwardness persists. Like the "Foreigner," every reader of epistolary fiction feels the pressure of certain "naive" questions having to do with the mediacy of the letter. Why do the characters write so much? How do they have time to *do* anything, if they are always writing letters? How have their letters been gathered together? Have they been edited? Who has put them in order? And so on. Yet such questions are really not so naive: they suggest the hermeneutic crux. The point is not, as one critic blithely puts it, that it is "silly to calculate how many hours a day characters must have had to spend scribbling."[5] The fact that we invariably do (even if secretly or intermittently) points to the unresolved difficulty in the form itself—one that ultimately undermines the mimetic contract with the reader.

Because it embodies, literally, a fictional history of its own production, the novel in letters constantly reminds the reader of the problem of origins. As mimesis, the epistolary form is uniquely self-defeating for just this reason: the more charac-

---

5. Mark Kinkead-Weekes, *Samuel Richardson: Dramatic Novelist* (Ithaca: Cornell University Press, 1973), p. 421.

ters refer to their own letter-writing activity—the act of production ostensibly mediating between the reader and the fictional world—the less *realistic* the fiction becomes. What Janet
Altman calls "epistolarity"—characters' allusion to the material side of correspondence (how letters are sent and delivered,
condition and quantity of pens and paper, the physical act of
composition, the nature of their handwriting)—perversely
serves to remind us of the very artificiality of the text's fiction
of its own origin.[6] The more one is forced to confront this
fiction, the more difficult it becomes to naturalize the
narrative—to fall into the illusion that the text is an objective
report, a history of real events, a representation of Nature.

Fredric Jameson suggests that the epistolary form inevitably
entails this breakdown of referentiality. The novel in letters,
he writes, always shows "a minute shift from the referential to
the literal, in which the letter writer calls our attention to his
own activity or to the words of his correspondent, to the *fact*
of writing itself. The effects of writing and reading are thus
promoted to the status of events within the novel, and end up
displacing the 'real' events which the letters were supposed to
relate."[7] This assertion is similar to Preston's point, noted
earlier, that in epistolary fiction "the process of writing, the

6. See Janet Altman, *Epistolarity: Approaches to a Form* (Columbus: Ohio
State University Press, 1981). *Sir Charles Grandison* is perhaps an even more
troubling example of the problems of epistolarity; for there, the self-
consciousness of the letter writers is, if anything, even more insistent than it
is in *Clarissa*. As well as the major correspondents, the novel also contains a
whole sub-bureaucracy of writers who contribute to the text—all the
amanuenses, memoranda-writers, and invisible "translators" (for the Italian
correspondents) Richardson must bring in now and then to keep the narrative going. Grandison, for example, sometimes has his conversations tran-
scribed by a secretary, then retranscribes his secretary's notes when he comes
to write his own accounts of the same conversations. If the epistolary convention makes *Clarissa* a hard book to read, in the case of *Grandison*, it makes
for a well-nigh *un*readable one.

7. Fredric Jameson, *The Prison-House of Language* (Princeton: Princeton
University Press, 1972), p. 200.

text itself, is the action." The reader can never really penetrate the textual surface, being constantly reminded of that activity of production which supposedly, yet improbably, brings it into being. One cannot escape into a world of experience "beyond" the world of correspondence. The reader's mimetic expectations are thus exposed and frustrated: for the subject of the writing seems no longer to be Nature, but textuality itself.

Just so, *Clarissa* confirms its own denatured status. This fact has disturbed some readers, particularly those whose critical lights lead them in a continual search after "Story"—an experiential realm existing somewhere beyond, or in spite of, the textual surface. Kinkead-Weekes, for instance—otherwise one of the most astute among Richardson's recent commentators—wants to maintain the mimetic illusion at all costs, even when the fiction itself will not allow him to do so. He recognizes the problem: "Richardson invites mockery because of the credibility gap between the bulk and frequency of the letters and our own experience as letter writers. . . . All art depends on convention, and all sensible criticism on recognizing and allowing for it. Yet because Richardson was a 'historian,' wedded to verisimilitude, he unwisely draws attention to the problem by fussing too much about it himself."[8] And he continues: "Necessary slabs of narration look even more awkward pretending to be letters"; the convention "creaks again whenever we see the tell-tale heading 'X—in continuation.'" But Kinkead-Weekes is impatient to move beyond the mediating device of the letter. He thus skirts the basic question of reading which it poses. Facing moments of obvious artifice, he recommends a kind of patronizing delicacy on the part of the reader—a willful determination not to notice. It is better, he writes, that we "tiptoe quietly past" the "clumsiness" of the epistolary form.[9]

8. Kinkead-Weekes, p. 423.
9. Kinkead-Weekes, p. 422.

But is such etiquette possible? Indeed *Clarissa* at times seems to force on us—even oppress us with—its artificial status. The tokens of epistolarity are omnipresent, everywhere thwarting our desire to plunge through the text toward "Nature." We cannot absorb meaning innocently. Though we may wish to naturalize the text—to view it passively as "History," as an assemblage of real letters written by real people about real events—such ultimately is an impossible task. At all points the question of origins emerges from the text itself, obstructing and discomfiting us, forcing us to consider the problematic epistemological status of the very fiction in which we try, with Clarissa-like purity, to believe.

The problem of origins is especially complicated in *Clarissa* because it intrudes simultaneously on two fronts—at a collective level, when we contemplate the text as a whole, and at a constituent level, when we examine individual letters. The Preface to *Clarissa* (prefixed by Richardson to the 1759 edition and reprinted in most modern editions) informs us, first of all, that what we are about to read is indeed a "History," "given in a Series of Letters." Immediately and unconsciously, we naturalize this claim to truth—accepting the fiction of historicity, suspending disbelief in order to proceed. Having once lured us on, however, with the promise of truth, the text suspends it—by repeatedly calling attention to the indeterminacy surrounding its own supposedly historical origin. Where has the great collage of writings, the "collection" itself, come from? The clues inside *Clarissa* remain disturbingly enigmatic and unsatisfying. At the end of the novel, we recall, Belford is collecting "packets" of letters from various persons; Clarissa herself entrusts him with letters she has received, and notes in her will that "Mr. Belford has engaged to contribute what is in his power towards a compilement to be made of all that relates to my Story" (VIII, 119). Yet nowhere is it clearly acknowledged that the collection we read is identical to the one Belford ostensibly makes, or that the editorial voice which occasionally interrupts the epistolary sequence, particularly in the last volume, with abrupt summations ("This collection having run into a much greater length than was wished, it is thought proper to omit several letters that passed between Colonel Morden, Miss Howe, Mr. Belford, and Mr. Hickman, in relation to the execution of the Lady's Will, &c." [VIII, 131]) is meant to be Belford's. Matters are rendered impossibly suspect in the later editions of *Clarissa* by the intrusion of the notorious "Richardsonian" editor, who appends footnotes, postscripted letter summaries, and so on, to the collection of letters itself. (We will return shortly to the other pernicious effects of Richardson's editorial additions.) All these interruptions work to destroy any illusion that *Clarissa* is in fact the edited "compilement" of papers relating to an actuality. The historicity of the "collection" is thrown into question, precisely because the text fails to generate any adequate explanation for its own existence, and instead subjects the reader to anonymous editorial voices that seem to have an inexplicable, yet privileged relation to the letters themselves.

Even if one tries, against the basic paucity of information, to maintain the fiction of the edited collection, there are still other problems. Have we indeed been provided with all the correspondence that relates to the heroine's "Story"? What has been left out of the numerous "extracted" letters? Anna Howe suggests to the dying Clarissa in one letter that her history be published at some point, but with "feigned names." Do we conclude that the names in the very "History" we read—in this ostensibly pure record of events—have in fact been changed? At the latter suggestion, the reader may very well feel a certain kinship with Clarissa herself: the possibility emerges that we do not know the *real* names of the correspondents in the collection, but like Clarissa at Mrs. Sinclair's, have been fooled by a succession of pseudonyms. Once again, our faith in the referentiality of the text is undermined.

It is when one considers the individual letter itself, how-

ever, that the antimimetic impact of the epistolary mode becomes even more blatant. The most primitive level of the
text—typography—works to enforce upon the reader a sense
of the artificiality of what he or she reads. And again, it is a
question of the problematic origin. Characters in *Clarissa* often
describe, for instance, the orthographic characteristics of their
writings and those of their correspondents. The "cut" of
Clarissa's letters, we learn from Anna, is "neat and free," and
her orthography everywhere distinguished by its "fairness,
evenness, and swiftness" (VIII, 223). When writing at moments
of duress or emotional intensity, writers frequently apolo-
gize for the shakiness of their pens, or the troubled shape
of their script. Such comments have a curiously subversive
effect on the real reader, however. Instead of assuring us of the
authenticity of what we read, they remind us precisely of the
inaccessibility of *original* documents, and our separation from
the realm of the "History" itself. The reader faces a disparity
between the handwritten artifact being described and the
printed text purportedly representing it. Inevitably, the disparity introduces a doubt, an anxiety, into our reading. It
exerts an unpleasant epistemological pressure. Is the printed
copy in our possession an accurate transcription (mimesis) of its
original? Is there, indeed, an *original*? We become aware that
we are at a potentially dangerous remove from truth, cut off
from an apparent actuality, the authentic letter.

Our anxiety increases at those moments when the typographic surface seems to flaunt its own ambiguous status. In the
case of Lovelace's and Belford's correspondence, for instance,
the reader confronts a veritable layering of artificiality. In
Volume III, Lovelace commands Belford that he write thence-
forth "in character, as I shall do to you" (III, 64). There are
later mentions of their "Algebra," or private shorthand; Belford writes at one point that he reads aloud Lovelace's letters
to Belton, Mowbray, and Tourville because "they can make
nothing of the characters we write in" (IV, 11). The real

reader, who can, of course, make everything of the characters they write in, is put in an uncomfortable position. For example, one may well be unpleasantly puzzled by those moments when the fiction later seems to forget the very information it has given us about this code: when Clarissa on her deathbed asks Belford for "a fair, a faithful Specimen" of Lovelace's letters to him, he obligingly sends her the most incriminating "Extracts" (VII, Letter 19), yet the text provides no evidence that these samples are the decoded transcriptions they must in fact have been. The truly "faithful Specimen," one remembers, is illegible. But the basic problem for the reader is that the portions of the text ostensibly written in the "Algebra" look just like all the rest of the text. We must try to imagine, when reading the Lovelace/Belford papers, that what we have before us is actually not just one, but two removes from the realm of *originals;* and that their letters have been deciphered by someone, as well as typographically reinscribed. Yet this very act of imagination is somehow too great to sustain; by forcing the reader to contemplate a particularly complicated, and again, mysterious process of transmission, the fiction casts doubt on its own epistolary premise. It simply asks us to do too much.

Similarly, when the complex interplay of forgeries is initiated midway in *Clarissa*, the reader is again apprised of the text's feigning. Just before forging one of Anna's letters Lovelace remarks that while he is able to mimic the friend's writing convincingly enough, he would not be able to do the same with Clarissa's own perfect hand. "Had it been my Beloved's hand, there would have been no imitating it, for such a length. Her delicate and even mind is seen in the very cut of her Letters" (v, 165). Once again, of course, it is precisely the "very cut" which, from the reader's point of view, is not "seen." The printed text has a leveling epistemological effect: it does not distinguish between the *forged* letter and the *real* letter. Our only evidence for forgery is intertextual. Ironically, we know that Lovelace indeed goes ahead to fake one of Clarissa's letters (v, Letter 15) despite his disclaimer, but we learn this only because he tells Belford so. Nothing in the printed version of the forgery signals its deceitful status—a fact that raises a disturbing question about the text of *Clarissa* as a whole. Is not the reader susceptible always—just as the heroine is—to unacknowledged forgeries? Are there others we don't know about? Once raised, the question dissolves, of course, into the greater realization: that indeed the entire text is a kind of forgery, that none of the letters are really authored by their supposed authors, but by a single invisible "pen." We recollect again the great sham at the heart of the text—the fiction of the mediating "letter" itself.

Finally, and most paradoxically, if *Clarissa* exposes its artificiality by its very inability to mime the physical details of the documents it purports to represent, on at least one perverse occasion it tries *too* hard to effect precisely this kind of mimesis. The result is typographic pathos. In the case of the notorious tenth "mad paper," written by Clarissa in her derangement, the typographic features meant to imitate her disordered orthography—the wrenched lines of type, words printed upside-down or askew—are so self-conscious, so comically intrusive, that we are simply reminded once more that we are not reading the *real* letter at all, but something else again. The pressure the typography exerts is enough to dissolve the mimetic pretense altogether. We are made so aware of the printed artifact—its poignant oddity, its hopeless failure to recall anything besides itself—that our faith in any original is breached. The text reveals itself here, paradigmatically, as nonreferential, autonymous, fantastical. It reveals itself as "Act."

The mediating device of the letter thus undermines in various ways the text's claim to "History." In its very intrusiveness, *Clarissa*'s epistolary medium blocks the reader's view of Nature. The technology of the letter usurps our gaze, and subverts the natural before our eyes, making us acutely conscious of the fictionality of what we read.[10] This might seem a fairly banal phenomenon. After all, one could ask, what reader of *Clarissa* has ever been *un*aware that the novel was indeed a work of "Art"? But the fact is we both know this and don't know it. In the abstract, at a distance from the text, we recognize that *Clarissa* is not really a "History," despite its pretense. In the moment of reading, however, our first move is always to forget what we already know. We sublimate both our awareness of the novel as an independent linguistic structure and our sense of ourselves as readers. One can speculate, of course, about the psychological compulsion at work here: the reader's attempt to naturalize the fictional world may reflect a basic desire to replace self-awareness with the impersonal plenitude of Nature itself. The wish to surrender to mimetic illusion perhaps conceals a wish to surrender the self: we seek in the act of reading a kind of temporary amnesia, an alternative to consciousness. This suspension of self, Bertrand Bronson has suggested, "is the characteristic joy of prose fiction, its promise, its potency, and its danger."[11] Yet *Clarissa*, complicated work of art that it is, repeatedly thwarts this will to sublimation. It brings us back to full knowledge, both of its own nature and our relation to it. The referential illusion

10. John Preston suggests that the printed page in *Clarissa* is a "form of mimesis." "[Richardson's] novel is not an imitation of life, but rather of writing." At the same time he claims somewhat paradoxically that Richardson purposely uses typography to subvert our mimetic expectations: "It is intended to keep before the reader the consciousness of being a reader. It is in fact a deliberate reminder of the unreality of writing" (Preston, *The Created Self: The Role of the Reader in Eighteenth-Century Fiction* [London: Heinemann, 1970], p. 46). One may question how deliberately Richardson sought to remind us of the sham nature of his own text, but Preston has indeed identified here the contradictory affect of the printed page: it at once presents itself as an image of written "documents," and exposes its own dissimilarity to these same documents.

11. Bertrand H. Bronson, "The Writer," in *Man Versus Society in Eighteenth-Century Britain*, ed. James L. Clifford (Cambridge: Cambridge University Press, 1968), p. 119.

disrupted, we are forced to recall the very process we so easily forget—reading itself.

There is a resemblance here, as I suggested before, between the process of demystification the reader of the fiction must undergo and the epiphanic progress of the heroine herself. We begin, as Clarissa does, ponderously naive—passive before the text, yet at the same time overwhelmingly curious. *Clarissa* seems to hold out a fascinating possibility of truth: we share the heroine's compulsion to interpret. Our wish is to interrogate the text, absorb it, register its truth within us. Yet if, like Clarissa, we want to read, we also share at the outset her primeval notions of what this process actually involves. The mimetic assumption is really a sort of willing hermeneutic fantasy: we grant that Nature itself has authorized the text, that Nature itself imbues it with meaning. In consequence, the task of the reader seems straightforward at first—a matter simply of consuming those meanings which arise *naturally* from the writing.

The realization that form itself enforces—that *Clarissa* is not in fact constrained by the nature of things, and that it has no historical claim on truth—is a shock not unlike the one Clarissa experiences when she discovers the basic deceit at the heart of her world. It is a powerful disillusionment. But it is also a provocation to inquiry. Like Clarissa after her "fall," we want information about the stratagem that has been executed against us. If the "Picture of Nature" is not indeed authorized by "Nature," whose act of "authority" does it then embody? And on what grounds must the search for meaning now proceed?

The reader's inquiry is not so easily resolved as Clarissa's. After her rape, the heroine soon recognizes and condemns the voluble "Intelligencer" responsible for her abuse. Lovelace is transparently behind it all—the "author," as she says, of her sufferings. Lovelace is an author on two counts: he has been the source of those mysterious and misleading texts which

Clarissa has rushed to interpret; he has inscribed her body itself with the marks of culpable "Womanhood" and treated her accordingly. Clarissa's recognition and subsequent denial of this dual "authority" over her person points to her new insight into the politics of meaning. She discovers at last that her own reading of the world has been as much an arbitrary "construction" as anyone else's. This is not to say that she has been free to believe whatever she wants: Clarissa's trauma indeed is the realization that meanings have been enforced upon her. Her comprehension of things has been neatly ordered from without, by an "Intelligencer." Lovelace has pro-scribed certain readings for her; he has written them out in advance, so to speak, in order to entrap her. Though not constrained, therefore, by "Nature," Clarissa's acts of interpretation have in fact been constrained by private tyranny. Playing "author" to Clarissa's "reader," Lovelace has controlled the domain of meaning itself.

The author/reader relationship in which the real reader is caught up, however, is not so simple. Who is the "Intelligencer" behind the deceitful text *we* read? Who controls us? The answers are not transparent. Certainly it is difficult to say with complacency, "Samuel Richardson." Richardson never impinges on us in the way that Lovelace impinges on Clarissa. Lovelace's role is described early on as that of a puppet-master, who "dances" other people on his "wires" (II, 27). And indeed, at the climax of his intimacy with the heroine, he is everywhere that she is, a *daemonic* presence: interrupting, anticipating, drawing her attention to what he wants her to notice, deftly distracting her from what he doesn't, stage-managing her existence—even while in disguise—through the sheer, outrageous intrusiveness of his person. Lovelace's "authority" depends upon a kind of avid contact with his "reader." He is a buttonholer and a haranguer: he exhorts Clarissa directly.

Richardson, in contrast, does no such thing with *his* reader. He can't. Strictly speaking, he is absent from us—invisible and inaudible, missing from the primary layer of his own text. (I mean by "primary layer," of course, the great "Series of Letters" itself, excluding for the moment the elaborate, bathetic editorial apparatus Richardson began adding in the second and third editions of *Clarissa*.) As we sift through the hundreds of letters, trying to piece together the semblance of a "Story," what we lack is precisely any sense of a controlling, magus-like authorial presence. We hear many voices, but none addresses us directly, in the way that gay and subtle Lovelace addresses Clarissa. None tells us what to believe.

Richardson, one could say, is not there when we need him most. And there are moments enough in *Clarissa* when we may long indeed for an author willing to dance us on his wires. Human actions in the novel often seem curiously overdetermined, by the text itself—hence their significance becomes ambiguous and puzzling. What are we meant to make, for instance, of Clarissa's "going off" with Lovelace? Her flight baffles, not because it is an intrinsically inexplicable event, but because it seems to have too *many* explanations. We receive no clue which, if any, is the right one. The text is too garrulous on the matter; we are given too many letters describing her motivation—too many "constructions" by different correspondents of the meaning of this crucial event. Clarissa's and Lovelace's disparate accounts make for the most perplexing dichotomy, of course. She tells Anna afterward that she "went off" because she feared the renewed terrorism of her relations: "Now behind me, now before me, now on this side, now on that, turn'd I my affrighted face, in the same moment; expecting a furious Brother here, armed servants there, an enraged Sister screaming, and a Father armed with terror in his countenance more dreadful than even the drawn sword which I saw, or those I apprehended. I ran as fast as [Lovelace]; yet knew not that I ran; my fears adding wings to my feet, at the same time that they took all power of thinking from me" (II, 359). Against this statement, however, we must later juxtapose a very different, indeed antithetical, interpretation of the flight. Lovelace hints broadly to Belford that Clarissa was not in fact impelled by fear of her family at all, but ran *to* him, out of the desire she won't acknowledge: "But seest thou not now (as I think I do) the wind-outstripping Fair-one flying *from* her Love *to* her Love?—Is there not such a game?—Nay, flying from friends she was resolved not to abandon, to the man she was determined not to go off with— *The Sex! The Sex, all over*—Charming contradiction— Hah, hah, hah, hah!" (III, 31). Charming contradiction, indeed. Nothing marks off one account as more privileged, or "truthful," than the other. (We discount absolutely, of course, those cultural prescriptions which encourage us in a male/female dispute to identify truth automatically with the male speaker.) Hence the reader's position is an awkward one. Without guidance, we must mediate between irreconcilables, channel an overflow of interpretative possibilities. Whether we incline toward Clarissa's or Lovelace's interpretation, or prefer instead an odd merger of the two or a new "construction" altogether, an element of doubt persists. Inevitably we remain conscious of the ultimate unverifiability of any judgment we may make about what *really* happened outside the garden wall at Harlowe-Place.

Such moments recur in *Clarissa* with alarming frequency.[12]

12. In "He Could Go No Farther: A Modest Proposal about Lovelace and Clarissa," *PMLA*, 92 (1977), Judith Wilt goes so far indeed as to suggest that Clarissa's rape is a nonevent. Wilt's "modest proposal" is that Lovelace is impotent and that what Clarissa actually suffers during the "black transaction" is mysterious sexual abuse at the hands of Mrs. Sinclair and the "women below." Wilt's view has been disputed (see R. Schmitz's response, *PMLA*, 92 [1977], 1005–6), but one must concede that nothing *in* the text definitively refutes it. Clarissa's account of her "usage" is decorous to the point of obfuscation, and Lovelace's hints afterwards to Belford that Clarissa may now be pregnant can—if impotence is indeed the issue—be seen simply as compensatory male-to-male bravado. I read *Clarissa* with the belief that a heterosexual rape does take place, with Lovelace as rapist, yet I am also aware that, technically speaking, this is as much a "construction" of what happens as is Wilt's revisionist proposal.

Again, it is the curious nature of the epistolary situation itself which makes for such indeterminacy. The occultation of "authority" we experience here—a sense of the absence of the author—is symptomatic of the classic novel in letters. As I noted briefly at the outset, the multiple-correspondent epistolary form, unlike other modes of narration, has no built-in authorial rhetoric. We hear no authorial voice in the text. For in order to create the fiction of the letter itself, the epistolary novelist must forfeit the storyteller *persona*, and abdicate overt responsibility for the fiction. He or she retains no power of utterance, no means of self-presentation—either of the direct (though ironic) sort we associate with the "Fielding" narrator of *Tom Jones*, or of the indirect, refracted sort Dickens achieves in *Great Expectations* through his narrative alter ego, the mature Pip.[13] The epistolary writer makes no personal contact with the reader; his or her identity, like that of the playwright, is displaced, hidden behind multiple *personae*. In contrast to the usual situation in first- and third-person narration, it is hard, thus, for the reader to generate an image of the author behind the text. Our access to the "implied author" (in Booth's famous term) is blocked by the form itself.

When the epistolary novelist foregoes the authorial *persona*, however, he or she also loses an essential means for exerting control over the reader. The choice of the letter form inevitably entails a weakening of authorial *power*. The very proliferation of fictional voices—the diffuse, babbling effect of correspondence—allows the reader a kind of participation and freedom not granted in other forms of narration. Above all, the reader is left to perform those basic organizational tasks

13. Booth's account in *The Rhetoric of Fiction* (Chicago: University of Chicago Press, 1961), of how authors using first- and third- person types of narration signal their intentions to readers and thus by degrees control interpretation has not been superseded. For an analysis of how Fielding constrains readers' moral responses through the use of a carefully designed authorial rhetoric, see also Sheldon Sacks's *Fiction and the Shape of Belief* (Berkeley: University of California Press, 1964).

which, in first- and third-person modes, are performed
paradigmatically (and with varying degrees of intrusiveness)
by a narrator: deciding, out of a mass of information, what is
significant to the "plot" and what is not, determining the physical, psychological, and moral displacement of characters, as-
sociating symbolic or thematic meaning with events in the
fictional world. The reader must take over the functions of the
storyteller, for the text itself supplies none. The reader shapes
the novel in letters into a coherent structure, and it is in this
sense, in Barthes's paradoxical language, that he or she
"writes" the text into being.

The absence of authorial rhetoric and the shifting of authority to the reader makes the classic epistolary novel marvelously
unfit, obviously, for didacticism of any kind. The epistolary
novelist can never express moral or social "messages" with the
relative precision and clarity available to a novelist using other
narrative forms. Though one character in the novel in letters
may, in effect, speak for the author and articulate authorial
points of view, this sanction can never be made apparent by
the epistolary sequence itself. The reader has no way of knowing, from the text alone, which correspondent is an authorial
mouthpiece. Thus we evaluate the moral significance of the
epistolary sequence as we wish, just as we "construct" the
story it ostensibly documents.

I distinguish here between the "classic" novel in letters—the
multiple-correspondent type, in which each letter writer is
given approximately the same amount of space in the text—
and epistolary novels such as *Pamela* or *Evelina*, in which the
letters of a single character (usually the heroine) tend to domi-
nate the sequence. The effect of the latter on the reader
gradually comes to resemble that of simple first-person narrative. Of *Pamela*—particularly the later sections of the novel,
where the letters turn into Pamela's "Journal"—Ian Watt has
noted that the effect is "not unlike that of the autobiographical

memoir in Defoe."[14] When letter upon letter follows with the "X—in continuation" heading and the replies are omitted, the reader's impulse is to read the letters as a continuous narrative, disregarding the breaks between them. To the degree that it approximates in this way a first-person memoir, the single-correspondent epistolary novel makes a far more successful vehicle for ideological statement than does the multiple-correspondent type. The dominant correspondent seems to speak with a special privilege and insistence—so much so that we tend almost invariably to identify his or her views with the real author's.

Thus in *Pamela*, for instance, the heroine's letters take over the epistolary sequence, until her voice becomes the sole voice of authority in the text—and virtually indistinguishable from Richardson's own. The result is a certain ideological over-simplification. Much of the interest of the novel, I think, lies precisely in the way the heroine's private discourse—which up to a point is basically spirited and self-respecting—modulates into a fairly embarrassing political statement: a paean to womanly subjugation—marriage with the "master." After Mr. B.'s proposal, Pamela's narrative—before, a clandestine, adversary speech—is usurped: it becomes the banal sign of her acceptance. Her powers of articulation are subsumed, taken over, and exist finally only in the service of this "master." She becomes, in short, a mouthpiece for those patriarchal values which have everywhere ordered her experience, and speaks a new discourse of subservience. The primary energy of the text (*Pamela* is nothing if not a convulsively *energetic* book) is directed toward, finally, the exorcism of tensions, the dissolution of thematic ambiguities, and the achievement of a rather garish kind of closure—the "comic" satisfaction of heroine and reader.

14. Watt, p. 209.

Clarissa in contrast offers little in the way of closure. It has more to do with fragmentation, difficulty, irresolution. One correspondent is always interrupted by another; no one viewpoint predominates. Specifically, the rigorously maintained symmetry between the Clarissa/Anna and Lovelace/Belford correspondences contributes perhaps more powerfully than any other formal detail of the text to its overall hermeneutic indeterminacy. The only satisfactions *Clarissa* proposes are tragic ones; it is much more mysterious.

Thus, in answer to our earlier question about *Clarissa* and meaning: the text bespeaks the final "authority" not of "Nature," not of Samuel Richardson, but of the reader. To enter the epistolary world is to confront an absence of natural and authorial constraints and to recognize one's own interpretative freedom. By virtue of its form, the text is neither convincing as mimesis or "History," nor can it masquerade as the *logos* of a single "Intelligencer." Instead, *Clarissa* emerges as a writing traced by the reader, as a function of exegesis itself. Penetrating the great "Series of Letters" is not so much, then, a matter of absorbing meaning from it, but of inscribing meaning upon it. The author is "dead," long live the author—the reader.

We do not dispense with history quite so easily, however; there is a final paradox left to us. Richardson himself does not seem to have intended or foreseen this "birth" of the reader—the very liberation his choice of form entails. Indeed, every claim he made for his "History" during and after its first publication suggests just the opposite: that he assumed it remained within the power of the epistolary novelist to pursue a great "end"—the moral indoctrination of the reader.

Richardson shared the view, conventional in his time, that the function of art was primarily didactic and the artist's role that of moral preceptor. In the "Author's Preface" to the 1759 edition of *Clarissa*, this didactic premise is inescapable: the goal of his own work, Richardson writes, is not simply to delight, but to teach. "Considerate Readers," he admonishes, "will not enter upon the perusal of the Piece before them, as if it were designed *only* to divert and amuse. It will probably be thought tedious to all such as *dip* into it, expecting a *light Novel*, or *transitory Romance*; and look upon Story in it (interesting as that is generally allowed to be) as its *sole end*, rather than as a Vehicle to the Instruction" (I, xv). The ideal reader Richardson imagines is one who sees *Clarissa* for what it is—an investigation "of the highest and most important Doctrines, not only of Morality, but of Christianity" (I, xv). In the claustrophobic Postscript to the same edition, he repeats nearly verbatim the words of the Preface, almost as if trying to enclose the text (and us) within the moral prescription: "It will, moreover, be remembered, that the Author, at his first setting out, apprised the Reader, that the Story (interesting as it is generally allowed to be) was to be principally looked upon as the Vehicle to the Instruction" (VIII, 328). The message is clear: the author communicates through his art; he offers us a moral teaching.

Critics often remark, more or less scurrilously, on the apparent disparity between Richardson's own understanding of what he was doing in his fiction—his express intentions—and the uncanny depths of meaning his works open up for the reader. I do not propose to enter here into a discussion of whether or not he was indeed, as some have claimed, an "unconscious" artist, who produced complex masterpieces without knowing that he did so.[15] But it must be acknowledged that Richardson seems often enough to have taken a singularly naive or else disingenuous view of his creations. Witness his surprise and chagrin at the cynical readings *Pamela* received, particularly Fielding's sly reinterpretation of the theme of

15. John Carroll summarizes the critical debate over Richardson's "unconscious genius" in his introduction to *Samuel Richardson: A Collection of Critical Essays* (Englewood Cliffs, N.J.: Prentice-Hall, 1969). On the same question see also B. L. Reid's "Justice to Pamela," *Hudson Review*, 9 (1956–57), 516–26, 533.

"Virtue Rewarded."[16] In the case of *Clarissa*, the purblindness is even more apparent. We have seen already that Richardson seems to have overestimated the mimetic potential of the "Epistolary Manner of Writing." Equally damagingly, however, he remained unaware—at least until it was far too late— of the destructive impact this same form has on the conventional author/reader dyad. Though committed ostensibly to "Instruction"—an ideal transfer of meaning from author to reader—Richardson chose in *Clarissa* the form least suited to didactic ultimatum. Authorial "Instruction" cannot coexist happily with readerly "construction"—yet it is this last operation that the multiple-correspondent epistolary novel requires.

Richardson either could not or would not see the hermeneutic paradox *Clarissa* embodied. A belated, partial recognition of the indeterminacy of his fiction came to him only gradually, after the first volumes of the novel had already appeared. He discovered then, to his dismay, that readers were responding to the text in ways dramatically at odds with his moral intentions. His pained reaction to what he perceived as misreadings of his book—notably by readers such as Lady Bradshaigh, who refused to see Lovelace as the "blackest of villains" and instead damned the heroine for her "over-niceness" regarding the marriage proposals—is well-documented. In a letter to Aaron Hill soon after the third and fourth volumes of the first edition appeared in 1748, Richardson complained of the tendency of his female readers in particular to yearn—inappropriately, he thought—for a "happy" ending: Lovelace's reformation, Clarissa's change of heart, marriage between them. "I intend another Sort of Happiness (founded on the Xn. System) for my Heroine, than that which was to depend upon the Will and Pleasure, and uncertain Reformation and good Behaviour of a vile Libertine, whom I could not think of giving a

16. See chap. 12, "The Reception of *Clarissa*: Richardson and Fielding 1748–1750," in T. C. Duncan Eaves and Ben D. Kimpel, *Samuel Richardson: A Biography* (Oxford: Oxford University Press at the Clarendon Press, 1971).

Person of Excellence to. The Sex give too much Countenance
to Men of this vile Cast, to make them such a Compliment to
their Errors. And to rescue her from a Rake, and give a
Triumph to her, over not only him but over all her Oppressors, and the World beside, in a triumphant Death (as Death
must have been her Lot, had she been ever so prosperous) I
thought as noble a View, as it was new. But I find, Sir, by
many Letters sent me, and by many Opinions given me, that
some of the greater Vulgar, as well as all the less, had rather it
had had what they call, an Happy Ending."[17]

There is a certain irony here: Richardson patronizingly as-
cribes to his female readers precisely that sort of flighty bad
judgment and sexual *faiblesse* that his heroine's fictional perse-
cutors belabor *her* with—and his remarks carry an unpleasant
burden of unacknowledged, almost Lovelacean misogyny.
Women readers who long for an ending in which Clarissa does
not die, he implies, are simply under the sway still of rakish
men, and must be corrected. It does not occur to him, obviously, that a female reader—even a moderately pious one—
might not necessarily take an unalloyed pleasure in seeing one
of her sex made over into a decomposing emblem of martyred
Christian womanhood, or respond wholly favorably to that
equation between sexual violation and death which he seems
unconsciously to have accepted as a given. Images of dead
or dying women were not quite so "new" as Richardson
imagined them; the early novels of seduction were after all
replete with them, and throughout the eighteenth century
(and beyond) visions of female disease and morbidity remained a literary commonplace.[18] Such images, one suspects,
may elicit somewhat different responses from the female and
male reader. In the case of Lady Bradshaigh—a fine and lively

17. Eaves and Kimpel, pp. 217-18.
18. See Nancy K. Miller, "The Exquisite Cadavers: Women in
Eighteenth-Century Fiction," *Diacritics* 5 (1975), 203-13, as well as Part II of
her book *The Heroine's Text: Readings in the French and English Novel 1722-1782*
(New York: Columbia University Press, 1980), "The Dysphoric Text."

woman—the desire to see Clarissa safely married off, even to Lovelace, seems to have been more a wish to nullify (in Nancy K. Miller's term) an unusually strong "dysphoric" response to Clarissa's dissolution than a sign of improper readerly predilections for the villain. As it stood, she wrote to Richardson, the death scene of Clarissa made her weep a "Pint of Tears" and throw herself on the floor in sympathetic "Agonies." "My Spirits are strangely seized, my Sleep is disturbed, waking in the Night I burst into a Passion of crying, so I did at Breakfast this Morning, and just now again." In a disturbing and obsessive act of identification, Lady Bradshaigh's reactions mimicked finally the fateful deprivation undergone by the heroine herself: "Something rose in my Throat, I know not what; which made me guggle as it were for Speech."[19]

One hesitates to defend the "greater Vulgar" on aesthetic grounds—a comedic resolution to *Clarissa* would undoubtedly have reintroduced, on a more massive and dreadful scale, that element of bathos which nearly sinks *Pamela*. But the rebellious responses of readers like Lady Bradshaigh dramatized from the outset the deeper problem inherent in Richardson's moralizing project. The "Series of Letters" did nothing, of course, to prevent such creative misreading or hold readers fixed on a single interpretative track. Rather it seems from the start to have invited precisely those kinds of "reconstruction" that wishful readers so eagerly supplied. It posed hermeneutic dilemmas that blended, vertiginously, into moral and ideological ones. No wonder struggling readers referred back, so transparently, to their own fantasies in order to sort out the "Story" and judge its characters.

Following this debacle, Richardson was no closer to appreciating that it was the form of *Clarissa* which led readers to entertain such profoundly different impressions of heroine, villain, and their respective actions. The pettishness of the letter to Hill was a bad omen: instead of accepting unexpected

19. Eaves and Kimpel, p. 224.

readings with equanimity, Richardson became convinced that a large number of his readers had willfully missed the point. Most important, he conceived a scheme to circumvent such unorthodoxy in future. In the subsequent editions of the novel, he began an elaborate rearguard action—that large-scale process of revision and alteration designed to obviate the problem of indeterminacy and establish, after the fact, his "authority" over his readers.

Modern readers bear witness, of course, to this sorry attempt. As William Warner reminds us in his detailed account of *Clarissa*'s publishing history in *Reading Clarissa*, twentieth-century editions, among them the standard Shakespeare Head and Everyman editions, incorporate most of the additions and changes Richardson began making in the second edition (1751) and completed in the third (1759). Thus as we read the novel today, we confront not only an epistolary sequence, but also the intrusive "editorial" apparatus Richardson added—the Preface and Postscript already mentioned, letter summaries at the end of each volume, an index of the work's "instructive sentiments" (referred to by Aaron Hill as that "Beautiful Compendium"), and most notoriously, a plethora of footnotes, in which Richardson, assuming the guise of "Editor," cross-references certain letters in the correspondence, supplies gratuitous information, and comments on events described by the letter writers.

Richardson's purpose in adding all of these extra features (which he less than candidly referred to as "restorations" to the text) is disarmingly clear: to institute precisely those "controuls" on reading which the letter sequence itself fails to supply.[20] By insinuating himself into the text as its editorial voice, Richardson tries, almost as an afterthought, to confine the

20. For a somewhat more sympathetic view of Richardson's editorial additions see the Bronson essay (n. 11 to this chapter). According to Bronson, Richardson is primarily attempting to maintain the traditional *personal* bond between author and reader which the proliferation of print media in the seventeenth and eighteenth centuries had drastically undermined.

meaning of Clarissa's "Story," to close off its gaps, and make it over as the pellucid fable of Christian heroism he desired that it should be.

Richardson tries to control us at every point in the reading process. The Preface, first of all, is a fairly ponderous attempt to condition our understanding of the letter sequence that follows. Thus Clarissa is promoted, even before we read her letters, as an "Exemplar to her Sex," endowed with "the noblest principles of Virtue and Religion" (I, xiii). In turn Lovelace, we learn, will stand as a dire refutation of "the dangerous, but too commonly-received notion, *that a reformed rake makes the best husband*" (I, xv). True enough perhaps this last—but also something of a foreshortening of *Clarissa*'s moral possibilities.

In each successive volume, however, Richardson works hard to make us accept the fictional world on just such simplistic terms. The most irritating form his propagandizing takes is undoubtedly the "editorial" footnote to the text. Like an ongoing, petulant babble at the bottom of the page, Richardson's notes intrude on our reading, calling attention—patronizingly enough—to "instances" of Clarissa's delicacy and Lovelace's infamy. By pointing up selected statements made by certain correspondents and ignoring others, the footnotes try to push us toward the "authorized" reading—Richardson's own. Richardson's tone is chiding, and, as Eaves and Kimpel note, he often falls into crude browbeating.[21] The repetitive formula, "The Reader will not have failed to notice," is one of his more annoying gambits—a stab at subtlety which barely hides his impatience to control the way we read and to check our anarchical impulses. Some of the notes, indeed, point to nothing more than Richardson's own mistrust of the reader, and his fear that *Clarissa*'s "Instruction" will continue to be ignored: "Surely those who have thought [Clarissa] to blame on

21. Eaves and Kimpel, p. 310.

this account, have not paid a due attention to the Story" (III, 13). "The particular attention of such of the Fair Sex as are more apt to read for the sake of the amusement, than instruction, is requested to this Letter of Mr. Lovelace" (III, 85).

The letter summaries at the end of each volume bespeak the same moral inflection and the same anxiety. By concealing implicit judgments of the fictional world in his synopses, Richardson less than innocently tries again to enforce on his audience a crude dichotomy between Clarissa's goodness and Lovelace's evil. Thus the saccharine description of one of the heroine's deathbed notes to Anna (VII, Letter 89): "A Letter full of pious reflections, and good advice, both general and particular; and breathing the true Christian spirit of charity, forgiveness, patience, and resignation. A just reflection, to her dear friend, upon the mortifying nature of pride" (VII, 485). Clarissa's actual letter is of course a much more complex and troubling affair—replete with hesitations and ambivalence, animadversions upon her "unsteady writing" and "trembling pen"—a marvel of ambiguity, in fact. It contains an excess of potential meaning, none of which Richardson's paltry, rigidifying abstract suggests. Richardson claims in his Preface that the appended summaries "enable the Reader to connect in his mind the perused volume with that which follows; and more clearly shew the characters and views of the particular correspondents" (I, xvi–xvii). But their function is ideological, rather than simply mnemonic or descriptive. They are corrective addenda, inelastic, meant to bring straying readers into line with the authorial position and establish the sanctimony of one interpretation.

Finally, the index of "Instructive sentiments" and the Postscript complete the exoskeleton of moralism. After we have finished reading the novel, the index refers us back to select moments in the text where, the "Editor" hints, we will discover "useful *theory* to the Youth of both Sexes" (I, xvii). Likewise, the Postscript summarizes once more the reading we are meant to make of *Clarissa*, and dismisses various objections lodged by readers of the first edition against the heroine's "exemplary" behavior.

The appalling irony in all of this is that Richardson's intrusions after the fact have an impact on us exactly opposite to what he seems to have intended. They incite readerly rebellion, rather than docility. More than heeding, we are inclined to resent such editorial "interruptions." Part of our response is due, I think, to Richardson's sheer heavy-handedness; so unsubtle are the attempts at control, readers with any independence of mind at all are inclined to bridle.[22] But the problem goes deeper than this. By putting artificial, external controls on how we interpret the epistolary world, Richardson acknowledges the problem with his text—that it indeed leaves matters of meaning to the reader, far too much so to suit an author committed to "Instruction." By their very existence, the editorial additions (particularly the ubiquitous footnotes) serve not as a set of constraints on reading but as patent reminders to the reader of his or her own freedom. With each addendum calling on us to organize the epistolary world in a certain way, we recollect our power to disobey "authority," and arrange it in *other* ways. If meaning were somehow transparent or intrinsic to the text—"natural," in other words—such superimpositions, we realize, would not be necessary. Yet the voice of the "Editor" proves the situation otherwise. It makes us conscious of the multiple liberties we can take.

In the attempt to reinstate his authorial prerogative, Richardson shows himself, paradoxically, as a less cunning "Intelligencer" than his own rakish creation. Had *he* been a

22. Kinkead-Weekes argues that Richardson's revision in the second and third editions "simplifies, and in doing so, distorts" the novel (p. 151). William Warner suggests that the appended letter summaries in particular attempt to formulate "a distinct interpretation of the novel," and constitute "the first critical essay written on *Clarissa*" (*Reading Clarissa: The Struggles of Interpretation* [New Haven: Yale University Press, 1979], p. 189).

"real" author, concerned with the "Instruction" of his readers, Lovelace of course would never been bothered with a form as intractable as the epistolary, nor would he have been happy with the ineffectual pose of "Editor." One might well imagine the sort of novelist Lovelace would have been: a third-person narrator à la Fielding or Thackeray—managerial, gay, complicitous and dramatic, confident of his power over his readers. It is interesting to note that the image associated with Lovelace, that of a puppet-master who dances his players on wires, reappears as the image the "Thackeray" narrator of *Vanity Fair* chooses for himself. In his Preface, we recollect, the latter describes himself as the "manager" of a puppet "Performance," and his comment on his heroine—"The famous little Becky Puppet has been pronounced to be uncommonly flexible in the joints, and lively on the wire"[23]—is a Lovelacean boast if ever there was one.

But Richardson seems not to have had the assurance for such direct assertions of "authority." He admitted always to an insecurity about assuming the role of narrator. Of *Clarissa* he wrote: "Some have wished that the Story had been told in the usual narrative way of telling Stories designed to amuse and divert, and not in Letters written by the respective Persons whose history is given in them. The author thinks he ought not to prescribe to the taste of others; but imagined himself at liberty to follow his own. He perhaps mistrusted his talents for the narrative kind of writing" (VIII, 325). One can speculate of course about the psychology of the author who chooses the epistolary form. The use of the letter device may indeed reflect—as it seems to have done in the case of Richardson—a personal insecurity about unmediated self-expression. By all accounts Richardson was an unusually, even annoyingly, meek and self-deprecating man. Aaron Hill said Richardson's only fault was his excessive "modesty."

23. William Thackeray, *Vanity Fair*, ed. J. I. M. Stewart (Baltimore: Penguin Books, 1968), p. 34.

Another acquaintance described him as a "silent plain man...
who seldom exhibited his parts in company... and who
heard the sentiments of others sometimes with attention, and
seldom gave his own." Richardson himself spoke to Lady
Bradshaigh of suffering from a "bashfulness, next to sheepish-
ness."[24] Because it offers the author a chance to impersonate
others directly, to speak in a displaced voice, the epistolary
form may well have appealed to Richardson's notably self-
effacing nature. Yet by opting for what he rationalizes as the
novelty of the epistolary style, Richardson abdicated from the
power he might have had. There is a posthumous quality to
the editorial additions to *Clarissa*—a belatedness that is felt by
the reader. By virtue of the epistolary form itself, Richardson
the author is dead to us, and the ghostly presence of
Richardson the "Editor" cannot take his place.

24. Eaves and Kimpel, pp. 520–21.

9

Epilogue:
The Reader Lives

The reader of *Clarissa* is free then—free of Nature, free of an "author." But what do we choose to do with our freedom? To what end this realization of readerly authority? The fiction itself seems at first to hold out two possibilities, both of them tragic. In the process of confronting the text, we discover, like the heroine herself, that it is the activity of interpretation which conditions meaning. The text itself is always fragmentary, mischievous; it never gives up the truth it promises. We thus impose a vision of Nature on it, rather than the other way around, and that which we read is only the inscription we have made. But this discovery involves us necessarily, it would seem, in a conscious power struggle with other exegetes: for in order to escape victimization, we are obliged to assert our reading of the text against the readings of others. To interpret, in the words of Anna Howe, is to affirm one's own "tyrant AUTHORITY"—to circumscribe, preempt, "interrupt" the other.

Faced with this Hobbesian vision of reading, Clarissa, as we have seen, opts for death. She refuses the implicit violence against the other that the act of "construction" entails; she ceases to read, and instead dies of "grief." And in a sense, the real reader of *Clarissa* is also free to "die." At any point in the text we may refuse to exert "authority" any longer, and simply stop reading. Many readers indeed never finish the novel, or can read it only in an abridgment. (Christopher Hill calls *Clarissa* "the greatest of the unread novels."[1]) *Clarissa*'s excessive length is part of its notoriety, of course, but it is not just a matter of length. The text repeatedly shifts responsibility for meaning to the reader, and for some this is too great a burden. The reader who reads simply to consume a predigested "Story" will be inclined to give up early on in *Clarissa*: it does not nourish in this way. Given the demanding nature of the fiction, the "suicide" of the reader is thus always a possibility; indeed, this is the metaphor at work in Dr. Johnson's famous observation that "if you were to read Richardson for the story, your impatience would be so much fretted that you would hang yourself."[2]

We have another choice, however, apart from this kind of self-abnegation. Lovelace is a reader from the start and remains one to the end. Though he knows it is false, and a work of "Art," he imposes his "construction" of the world on others; he asserts his readings with the necessary "force." Rather than follow Clarissa into death—the death that is the end of interpretation itself—the reader may plunge with Lovelace into hermeneutic struggle. Historically, most of *Clarissa*'s greatest critics have done just this—presenting readings of the work, becoming partisans of one sort or another, usually on the side either of the heroine or Lovelace himself. The history of much Richardson criticism, as I suggested at the outset, is a recapitulation of the very kind of interpretative struggle going on in the fictional world—a succession of readings, all equally arbitrary (in the sense that none can claim an epistemologically

1. Christopher Hill, "Clarissa Harlowe and her Times," *Essays in Criticism*, 5 (1955), 313.
2. James Boswell, *Life of Johnson* (London: Oxford University Press, 1969), p. 480.

privileged relation to the text, which is indeterminate), yet all contesting and rewriting one another.

Are the choices Clarissa and Lovelace make, however, really so distinct? And do they represent, indeed, an end to possibility for the real reader? I described both as being finally tragic options. Clarissa's decision not to read at all is a literal death, of course, but the Lovelacean struggle to continue reading also ends in death—his slaughter at the hands of Clarissa's avenger Colonel Morden. We need to reemphasize that *Clarissa* dramatizes a *politics* of meaning, and within the tragic fictional world, this politics is invariably linked to a kind of fatality. As much as anything, Clarissa's final despair is a political despair—a recognition that she has not the power to articulate her reading of the world. As "Child" to the Harlowes, as "Woman" to Lovelace, she has no defense against the kinds of interruption she suffers. Thus, though in one sense she seems voluntarily to forego hermeneutic struggle, in another she has no choice: she remains a victim of the politics of "authority." Lovelace is another sort of victim; he survives longer, triumphing over the heroine because, being party to traditional masculine prerogatives, he is free to exercise a set of social, economic, psychological, and sexual "controuls" over her. But he too ultimately falls victim to the "authority" of another. Succumbing to Morden's martial "force," Lovelace succumbs to a system of meanings more powerful than his own, for the Colonel carries the symbolic weight of patriarchal law behind him—the very law Lovelace has broken by ravishing the heroine. (Strictly speaking, Morden's revenge is not so much on behalf of Clarissa, but on behalf of the Harlowe males, whose property rights Lovelace has violated by "stealing" her.[3]) Lovelace's own death (which is a kind of "penetration") is actually as political as that of the woman he persecutes.

3. See Susan Brownmiller on the economic significance of early rape statutes, *Against Our Will: Men, Women, and Rape* (New York: Simon & Schuster, 1975), pp. 15-19.

But this is a grim picture. We may feel uncomfortable at the thought that this same fatality informs our own interpretative operations. Yet to assert the validity of an interpretation—of the fiction, of the world—is to engage, at least symbolically, in exactly the sort of deathly contest that *Clarissa* thematizes. Traditionally, literary criticism has been founded on such violence, though sublimated. New readings of a given work typically affirm their claim on truth by destroying previous readings, often through that kind of fragmentation represented by incriminating, "Lovelacean" citation. Likewise, commonly accepted, "successful" or "standard" readings of a work have most often been those which implicitly replicate the ideology of a larger political power structure—typically, that of the academic institution which fosters them, or of society itself.

In *Clarissa* criticism, the treatment accorded the heroine's rape has been just such a case in point. Before the rise of feminist critical theory—which itself reflects a relative consolidation of women's power in the academic community and in society—few critics regarded Clarissa's violation with any direct opprobrium. Those commentators who did sympathize with her usually did so more on the grounds that she represented a species of Christian martyr, than because they saw her as a victim of sexual violence. In turn her detractors—similar in spirit to the "anti-Pamelists"—often suggested that in one way or another she had "asked for it" by behaving unsuitably or ambiguously.

Ian Watt's otherwise classic statement on *Clarissa* is marred by a tendency toward a "Lovelacean" reading of Clarissa's character in this regard. Though he acknowledges that "opinions may well vary" about her rape, he seems to have a fairly clearly formulated view of how it comes about: "Unconsciously, no doubt, Clarissa courts sexual violation as well as death." Watt believes that a "masochistic fantasy" underlies Clarissa's entanglement with Lovelace—a desire for "desecration" at the hands of the "sadistic and sexual male." Her death wish, he suggests, may in part arise from an awareness that in the matter of the assault upon her "she herself is not wholly blameless." Watt distances himself from this masculinist "construction" of the novel by claiming that the Clarissa/Lovelace relation embodies "the dichotomisation of the sexual roles in the realm of the unconscious" and a "conceptualisation of the sexual life" characteristic of Western culture.[4] Yet in assuming automatically that Clarissa "courts" violation—when her behavior may be explained with equal plausibility not in terms of a subliminal "desire" for rape, but in terms of a desire for articulation—Watt seems to fall victim to the very sexual mythology he seeks elsewhere to demystify.

Such readings turn finally upon traditionally sanctioned masculine attitudes, and reflect the fact that *Clarissa*'s critics have been themselves mostly male and sometimes insensitive to the sexual politics of Lovelace's act. With the recent (slight) change in social attitudes regarding rape, the feminist critic can now pose a different "construction" of the event, but must still contest with earlier entrenched misogynist readings. To borrow Harold Bloom's term, the "strongest" reading of a work remains that which, invoking the authority of the moment, can defeat its opposite. And the strongest reader is still the one who can interrupt the other, the one who risks "death" successfully in the critical arena and thus enforces his or her desire.

I would like to suggest, however, that while *Clarissa* indeed dramatizes just such a tragic world of interpretation, it also intimates the possibility of escape. Unlike Clarissa and Lovelace, the real reader is offered a kind of *life* unavailable to those caught up in hermeneutic struggle, a chance at catharsis.

The possibility of catharsis arises precisely from that very self-consciousness the fiction entails upon us. By its form

4. Ian Watt, *The Rise of the Novel* (Berkeley: University of California Press, 1957), pp. 231-33.

Clarissa engages us in a paradox: we are both in and out of reading. We at once witness a reading process and read ourselves. But by documenting so clearly *within* the fictional world the arbitrariness of readings, the intimate connection between interpretation and violence, meaning and power, *Clarissa* challenges us to reflect upon our own hermeneutic project, beginning with that very act of "penetration" we try to perform with regard to the text itself. The text, as we have seen, continually reinforces this self-awareness by suspending those conventions by which we are accustomed to recuperate fictional works, thus exposing before us the productive nature of our own interpretative enterprise. We are forced to confront, therefore, our "authority," specifically in light of those acts of hermeneutic aggression taking place in the fictional world.

Yet our peculiarly split consciousness is also potentially liberating, for we are encouraged, in a way that none of the fictional readers is, to analyze reading itself. By presenting to us the history of various "constructions" within the fictional world—their grounding in desire and power—*Clarissa* encourages us to consider the grounds upon which we perform our own acts of "construction." What images of the "natural," what hidden ideologies, what sublimated wishes constrain the way *we* look at the text—or indeed, at the world? How do we let other readers or our own previous readings inform our interpretative decisions? And how do our readings impinge on others? *Clarissa* raises such questions, and thus points us toward an examination of that larger political context in which exegesis always takes place—the context of desire and conflict. The text invites us, insistently and radically, not simply to read, but to read our own reading—to turn it back on itself.

The subversive force of *Clarissa*, finally, is that it leaves the real reader free to envision a critical discourse not founded on the death of the other. When we forego the articulation of a particular reading, and instead try to articulate the motives for reading itself, we demystify the process and begin to nullify its violence. This demystification could, I suppose, ultimately be called a kind of moral action; for when we take interpretation itself for our subject, our subject is no longer the other, but ourselves. Unlike Lovelace inscribing Clarissa's "Nature" according to the infamous "Rake's Creed," we inscribe the nature of the creed itself, and begin thus—not a history of the other—but a history of our own desires. It may be that this new discourse must remain in some sense an ideal one. In my own analysis, for instance, though I have tried to avoid "construction" and instead simply follow out the text's revelation of this process, I have found myself nonetheless making pleasing arrangements of the fictional world, abrading the textual surface, interpreting always. Still, in that *Clarissa* allows us to imagine a history of reading, it grants us a certain cathartic knowledge. In attempting to articulate this knowledge, it is *Clarissa*'s reader, and not its silenced heroine, who in the end, lives.

Bibliographic
Postscript

Since the 1950s about the only thing that has united *Clarissa*'s often radically divergent commentators has been the desire for "Story"—the wish to extract from the text a *mythos*, a symbolic plot, a system of meanings of one sort or another. It is not my purpose here to offer an exhaustive summary of *Clarissa* criticism, but simply to remind the reader that the different "constructions" placed on Richardson's great, balky text have been exactly that: images of order imposed from without by readers. In pursuit of *Clarissa*'s meaning critics may differ in the particular critical vocabularies they invoke in order to decode the fiction (and in the degree of intimacy they claim to have with Richardson's conscious intentions), but the overriding project is the same: to produce an interpretative structure within which all elements of the novel may be contained.

One can make rough divisions among typical sorts of readings *Clarissa* has received in the last few decades. Traditionally, a number of critics have interpreted the novel on intentionalist grounds, giving privileged importance to Richardson's own sense of his work and his audience. His recent biographers T. C. Duncan Eaves and Ben D. Kimpel are a case in point. By relying on a close reading of Richardson's letters and subsequent remarks on *Clarissa*, they construct a reading of the novel very similar to his own, in which subliminal or subversive moral and psychological possibilities are discounted and Clarissa's exemplary qualities are stressed. "A reader might well ask himself as he reads whether he is not caught up in Clarissa's reality to see through her eyes and whether as he does so he is not moved to a sort of admiration, a sense of the possibilities and powers of the human spirit" (*Samuel Richardson: A Biography* [Oxford: Oxford University Press at the Clarendon Press, 1971], p. 277). Eaves and Kimpel have disparaging words for those readers who unearth meanings not acknowledged by Richardson himself or by contemporary readers: "Readers who find abstract statements about social relationships or illustrations of the doctrines of psychoanalysis of primary interest may read *Clarissa* in the light of one of these myths or, if they are clever enough, make up their own. We will discuss the novel, as Richardson's simple contemporaries (including Diderot and Johnson) read it, in terms of its realistic surface" (p. 241). Mark Kinkead-Weekes (*Samuel Richardson: Dramatic Novelist* [Ithaca: Cornell University Press, 1973]), Margaret Doody (*A Natural Passion: A Study of the Novels of Samuel Richardson* [London: Oxford University Press at the Clarendon Press, 1974]) and Cynthia Griffin Wolff (*Samuel Richardson and the Eighteenth-Century Puritan Character* [New York: Archon Books, 1972]) share in varying degrees the intentionalist bent, recuperating the fiction primarily in terms of Richardson's express artistic, moral, and religious concerns. Jean Hagstrum's recent discussion of the ideology of love and sex in the novel—in *Sex and Sensibility: Ideal and Erotic Love from Milton to Mozart* (Chicago: University of Chicago Press, 1980)—is likewise founded on the premise that Richardson in some sense speaks through his work, and embodies in it those assumptions about heterosexual passion which he shared with his contemporaries. Alan Wendt's much anthologized piece, "Clarissa's Coffin," *Philological Quarterly*, 34 (1960), 481–95, reinforces Richardson's notion of his heroine as the representative of "the great doctrines of Christianity," as does Gerard A. Barker's essay "The Complacent Paragon: Exemplary Characterization in Richardson," *Studies in English Literature*, 9 (1969), 503–19.

Other critics, in contrast, have been less willing to organize *Clarissa* according to Richardson's own prescriptions and didactic concerns, and instead have made claims for implicit nonintentional sorts of significance in the novel. The classic statements of Ian Watt in *The Rise of the Novel* (Berkeley: University of California Press, 1957) and Christopher Hill in "Clarissa Harlowe and Her Times," *Essays in Criticism*, 5 (1955), 315–40, describe Clarissa's "Story" primarily in sociological terms: *Clarissa* is significant mainly as revelation of bourgeois ideology—social, economic, and sexual. Similar interests inform, of course, the famous analyses of *Clarissa*'s "myth" critics, Leslie Fiedler and Dorothy Van Ghent, who claim for it an underlying archetypal meaning. (See Fiedler, *Love and Death in the American Novel* [New York: Stein and Day, 1960, rev. ed. 1966], and Van Ghent's chapter on *Clarissa* in *The English Novel: Form and Function* [New York: Holt, Rinehart, & Winston, 1953].) Both Fiedler and Van Ghent locate paradigmatic psychosexual significance in the fiction: *Clarissa* is, above all, a mythic statement on the paradoxical Western fascination with and fear of heterosexual relations. Morris Golden's work, finally, proposes an intrinsic psychoanalytic content for the fiction. He is concerned to interpret *Clarissa* in the light of theories of sado-masochism, and to see in it a symbolic revelation of Richardson's own (unconscious) fantasies of dominance and submission. See *Richardson's Characters* (Ann Arbor: University of Michigan Press, 1963).

No matter whether it thematizes a didactic, sociohistorical, psychological, or archetypal content, the traditional single reading of *Clarissa* almost invariably implicitly excludes or tries to discount other interpretative possibilities. Few of the foregoing commentators acknowledge critical pluralism or make a case for the polysemousness of the text. Typically, *Clarissa*'s commentators naturalize their own readings—that is, identify them, exclusively, with truth itself. The same phenomenon is played out even when critics appear to share a similar critical vocabulary or methodology. Most recently, Katharine M. Rogers, in "Sensitive Feminism vs. Conventional Sympathy: Richardson and Fielding on Women," *Novel*, 9 (1975), 256–70, and Judith Wilt, in "He Could Go No Farther: A Modest Proposal about Lovelace and Clarissa," *PMLA*, 92 (1977), 19–32, both claim a feminist perspective on the novel yet construe it radically differently. One sees it as an example of "sensitive feminism" and the other as an unpleasantly antifeminist document (cf. Wilt, p. 267). Each "construction" nevertheless makes its rhetorical claims on truth.

Only very recently has the "constructive" approach to *Clarissa* been challenged by what one could call a "deconstructive" one: John Preston's chapter on *Clarissa* in *The Created Self: The Reader's Role in Eighteenth-Century Fiction* (London: Heinemann, 1970), Leo Braudy's "Penetration and Impenetrability in *Clarissa*," in *New Aspects of the Eighteenth Century*, ed. Phillip Harth (Essays from the English Institute) (New York: Columbia University Press, 1974), and William B. Warner's work are not so much interpretations of the novel as examinations of the way it thematizes interpretation itself. My own study is a further attempt at this sort of investigation.

Because our work on *Clarissa* shares certain methodological assumptions, and in some respects invites comparison, I would like to conclude this essay with a few remarks in particular about William Warner's treatments of *Clarissa*—his article "Proposal and Habitation: The Temporality and Authority of Interpretation in and about a Scene of Richardson's *Clarissa*," *boundary 2*, 7 (1979), 169–99, and *Reading Clarissa:*

The Struggles of Interpretation (New Haven: Yale University Press, 1979). In *Reading Clarissa* (which came to my attention as I finished the first draft of this book), Warner writes that his reading has been "informed and molested by the theoretical questions addressed in the texts of Nietzsche, Derrida, Barthes, and others" (p. ix). I agree entirely with his basic premise, eloquently presented, that "the textual field of *Clarissa*, with its intricate history, is like a vast plain where Clarissa and Lovelace, and their respective allies, and the two ways of interpreting the world they embody, collide and contend" (p. viii). Likewise, we share a view that "the struggles of interpretation between Clarissa and Lovelace 'inside' the book are always already part of the struggles of interpretation that go forward 'outside' the book" (p. ix).

What remains surprising and disturbing about Warner's study, however, is that while he supports the idea that meaning is never immanent in a text, but is always constituted by the reader in response to the text (and indeed that the meaning of *Clarissa* itself has been repeatedly "delivered" by its subsequent readers, including notably Richardson himself), he seems unaware of the political dimensions of hermeneutic struggle. The battles of interpretation, in the text, in the world, are seldom fair fights. In the case of *Clarissa*, it is true that Clarissa and Lovelace "collide and contend" in their efforts to affirm their "constructions" of experience and each other, but they are nowhere equal combatants in a political sense: Lovelace has available to him a kind of "force" Clarissa does not—all the institutionalized advantages of patriarchal power, including the power of sexual intimidation. The long series of "interruptions" Clarissa is subject to on account of her sex and status—and above all the overwhelming fact that she gets *raped* for trying to articulate (something that Lovelace never has to worry about)—are of little moment to Warner. Warner is right to see in *Clarissa* a paradigmatic exposure of the "question of authority" (p. x), but what he does not see is that this exposure raises political as well as epistemological issues.

Thus his study modulates too often into a barrage of ill-considered attacks on Clarissa and boyish expressions of admiration for Lovelace—all of which rest upon an implicit sexual politics he never stops to examine. Characteristically Warner blames the woman, Clarissa, for the very action ("construction") he praises in the man, Lovelace. Because she tries to articulate her own "Story"—to control the way she is understood by others, and thus arrive at "the moment of achieved meaning" (p. III)—Clarissa becomes for Warner a "suffocating" or "claustrophobic" presence in the text, one who "induces anger and irritation—and a profound itch for an entirely new wave of sentiment" (p. 113). Lovelace on the other hand (whose rights to articulation and "Story"-telling go unquestioned) is "a brilliant elaborator of fictions" (p. ix). The spirit of Nietzsche (and *his* complaint against "Woman") hangs unpleasantly over this adjudicating: Warner condemns Clarissa for subtly "aggressive" and "irreducibly self-centered" attempts to present her view of things (p. 38), and claims her acts of "construction" reek of "self-present virtue" (p. 36). Yet the same acts performed by Lovelace are "charming" (p. 51), "playful" (p. 49), and ultimately become "unselfconscious expressions of his need for another" (p. 38). "Lovelace's art can coexist with a surprising degree of directness, honesty, and attachment" (p. 38).

At times Warner's anti-Clarissaism, and the startlingly primitive misogyny that seems to underlie it, become simply embarrassing—as when, in a revealing burst of rhetoric, he hints that Clarissa is perpetually "hiding something unsavory beneath her garments" (p. 26), that is, concealing her "manipulative" strategies against others. Likewise they provide him with a rationale for rape: Clarissa's self-present virtue needs "displacing," "disturbing," "subverting," "undoing" ("Lovelace and the Stages of Art"). Women readers in particular may be surprised to hear that Lovelace's "way of operating," which culminates ("logically," Warner suggests) in sexual violence, "engenders something shared and mutual" (p. 38). (It is not insignificant that Warner thinks of *Clarissa*'s reader and his own reader always as a "he.")

What Warner seems unable to accept is the possibility, implictly raised, though never fulfilled in *Clarissa*, of power located in a *female* voice. Such power, he assumes, must "necessarily" be dis-located. This in itself is an unacknowledged ideological stance, and one that results, finally, in a severe distortion in the last part of his book. There he launches into a spirited "deconstructionist" attack on *Clarissa*'s "humanist" critics—all those, from Richardson himself (in his editorial role) to Watt, Doody, "Woolf" (*sic*), and Kinkead-Weekes, whom he claims have complicitously supported the heroine's cause by granting privileged status to her values, the values of the "humanist sublime," including: "seriousness, consistency, sympathy, maturity, a full deep heart," and above all, "belief in the 'real'" (p. 268). The truly radical, deconstructive reader, he implies, must needs be Lovelacean, for to belong to "Clarissa's party" is automatically to invest one's own discourse, bathetically, with this transparently mythological "humanism." What Warner misses is that it is possible to speak for Clarissa without adhering to her (or Richardson's) specific values, without advocating her "apotheosis" as Christian heroine (p. 269), without invoking simplistic humanist notions of the "real." One can allow with Warner that her "narrative" (what there is of it) is "not impartial" (p. 267) and yet still view her for what she is—a political victim. And it is equally true that one can experience Lovelace—with his endless yammering on about the "Rake's Creed" and the nature of "Woman"—as a "suffocating" and "claustrophobic" textual presence, without sacrificing one whit of one's poststructuralist consciousness. For *Clarissa* dramatizes not only the "constructive" nature of the real, but the patterns of victimization and abuse that occur when meanings are arbitrarily inscribed and reinscribed. And as Barthes has pointed out in *Mythologies* and elsewhere, though as readers of the text we may no longer concern ourselves with a dynamics of "truth" and "falsehood," we can still concern ourselves—both within the text and without—with the dynamics of oppression.

Index

INDEX

rape, 25–26, 166n12
  as articulation, 114
  and ideology of male supremacy,
    117, 185
  relation to hermeneutic theme,
    108–117
  and textual violation, 111–113,
    121
  treatment in *Clarissa* criticism,
    117n3, 184–85, 194–95
  See penetration
reading, 19–20, 47–56, 148–180
  bipartite form in epistolary fic-
    tion, 40–43
  cathartic possibilities in, 185–87
  as construction, 21–22, 45, 53,
    141–42, 165, 189
  model for interpretation of ex-
    perience, 50–54
  and penetration, 77, 111–14,
    138–39, 144
  as productive activity, 20–21,
    27–28, 51–56, 71, 87
  relation to writing, 48–50
  and violence, 22–23, 71–72, 86,
    108–18, 181–83
  See also authority; epistolary form;
    interpretation; letters; pene-
    tration
Reid, B. L., 171n15
Rich, Adrienne, 31
Richardson, Samuel, 148–80
  correspondence with Lady Brad-
    shaigh, 49
  editorial role in *Clarissa*, 158,
    175–78
  on epistolary form, 50, 152–53,
    179
  Hints of Prefaces for Clarissa, 50
  on moral function of fiction,
    170–71
  Pamela, 168–69, 171
  psychology, 179–80

relations with readers, 171–75,
    178–79
revisions of *Clarissa*, 158, 175–80
Sir Charles Grandison, 155n6
views on *Clarissa*, 17, 27, 171–72
Robbe-Grillet, Alain
  Les Gommes, 75
Rogers, Katharine M., 192
Rosbottom, Ronald, 42, 43, 44n9,
    59

Sacks, Sheldon, 167n13
Sade, Marquis de, 23, 24
Sale, William, 30, 39
Scripture, 129–31
  as sanction for misogyny, 87–88
  vulnerability to editorial violence,
    131
sexual roles
  conventionality of, 75
  inversion of, 74–76, 98–100
Shklovsky, Viktor, 76
signs, 81–107
  alimentary, 53, 91, 106–7, 125–
    26
  bodily, 49, 69–70, 88–89, 104–7,
    110–11
  graphemic, 143
  heraldic, 100, 101–2
  iconographic, 139, 142–44
  linguistic, 66–69, 73, 91–95,
    126–35
  literary, 84–86
  sartorial, 91, 102–4, 111, 124–25
  topographic, 101
  See also cipher; interpretation;
    reading
silencing, 22–23, 62–66, 114–19
  of female utterance, 30–31, 63n3,
    115
  and rape, 114–15
  See interruption
Spacks, Patricia Meyer, 20

200

CLARISSA'S CIPHERS

Designed by G. T. Whipple, Jr.
Composed by The Composing Room of Michigan, Inc.
in 11 point VIP Janson, 2 points leaded,
with display lines in Janson.
Printed offset by Thomson-Shore, Inc.
on Warren's Number 66 text, 50 pound basis.
Bound by John H. Dekker & Sons, Inc.
in Holliston book cloth
and stamped in Kurz-Hasting foil.

Library of Congress Cataloging in Publication Data

CASTLE, TERRY.
  Clarissa's ciphers.

  Bibliography: p.
  Includes index.
    1. Richardson, Samuel, 1689–1761.   Clarissa.
  2. Women in literature.   3. Reader-response criticism.
  Title.
PR3664.C43C37   1982   823'.6   82–2460
ISBN 0–8014–1495–4   AACR2